WORK, LOVE, PLAY

Self Repair in the Psychoanalytic Dialogue

Joel Shor

BRUNNER/MAZEL, *Publishers* • NEW YORK

Library of Congress Cataloging-in-Publication Data
Shor, Joel
    Work, love, play : self repair in the psychoanalytic dialogue /
Joel Shor.
        p.   cm.
    Originally published: Los Angeles, Calif. : Double Helix Press,
1990.
    Includes bibliographical references.
    ISBN 0-87630-658-X
    1. Psychoanalysis—Philosophy.   2. Psychotherapist and patient.
3. Humanistic psychotherapy.   I. Title.
    [DNLM: 1. Professional-Patient Relations.   2. Psychoanalytic
Therapy.   WM 460.6 S559w 1990a]
    RC509.S54   1992
    616.89'17—dc20
DNLM/DLC
for Library of Congress   91-36576
                                                               CIP

Published by
BRUNNER/MAZEL, INC.
19 Union Square West
New York, New York 10003

Manufactured in the United States of America

10 9 8 7 6 5 4 3 2 1

Contents

*A series of essays on ethics for negotiation, empathy
and interpretation in psychotherapy*

A Note by Marion Milner

This important book will be useful to all students in training to become psychotherapists or psychoanalysts, as well as to their teachers. It will also prove informative—and accessible—to lay people interested in what is happening after so many years to Freud's original discoveries.

Tracing this scholar-clinician's progress from, at the age of 21, refusing the advice of a famous senior analyst that he should begin by undertaking medical training to becoming a much-valued faculty member of the teaching staff at the Harvard Medical School Department of Psychiatry, the book serves as both a compelling personal journal and an historical overview of the field.

In the book Dr. Shor describes his work with a number of the distinguished analysts who had come from Freud's circle in Vienna, and also what he gained or rejected from them. He recalls Freud's statement that his aim for patients was to help them to achieve the capacity to work and to love. To this, Dr. Shor adds the capacity to play, thus being in agreement with D. W. Winnicott. Central to his perspective is the certainty that the analyst does not know better than the patient, his function being to provide the safe space in which the patient can find that within himself that makes for healing, both for self-repair and repair of his relationships.

The feeling one gets in reading the book is that here is someone with a profound respect for that unique something that we call a person, and for that deep mysteriousness or whatever it is that makes for personhood; also a willingness to share in detail how he has slowly learned to express that respect in a totally nonauthoritarian dialogue with his patients.

MARION MILNER
Training Analyst
British Psycho-Analytic Society

Foreword

There is a puzzling paradox in psychoanalysis: that system of theory and practice which centrally aims at liberation of the human mind has recurrently been on the brink of falling into dogma itself. Its adherents, although generally admitting that we are far from having arrived at ultimate truths, nevertheless tend to keep vigilant watch lest those within its ranks depart from received beliefs and clinical techniques. Such persons are at best regarded as 'revisionists' and at worst as heretics to be excommunicated from the realm. Thus many psychoanalytic institutes are riddled with tensions, and, at least in the United States, their histories are replete with splits. Some of the diminishing influence of Freud's thinking in our universities and in clinics and hospitals today may be attributed to the relatively rigid ways in which the followers of the founder have applied his ideas. Yet perhaps the miracle is that, in spite of the prevalence of doctrinaires in our midst, psychoanalysis does manage to develop and to flourish, to build on the rich heritage which Freud bequeathed us, and indeed to become a many splendored thing.

This book is an account of one analyst's half century of learning and applying clinically what he has learned. When he presented some of this material at a psychoanalytic meeting, he was accused of being a 'radical humanist,' an epithet with which he does not quarrel. By his own admission, this writing is 'flagrantly ethical' in its emphasis, its fierce defense of the individual human being and his/her capabilities and of the rights of each person to freedom for self-determination. His attacks on the authoritarian element which sometimes creeps into psychoanalysis will not be welcome in some quarters, but fortunately he is not alone for there are a number of other voices being heard, in general medicine as well as in psychiatry and psychology, which declare for the patient's being a more active participant in whatever treatment approach. Shor bases his central principle on Freud's own statement that the patient must be *in charge* of all aspects of the therapy,

In these pages the author interweaves his own professional history with the development of his ideas to the present, showing us the influences along the route. One has the impression that not much was left to chance, for Shor seems to have been a restless seeker, ever aware that what he knew at any given time was not good-enough, so that he was propelled into many moves to emend theories and practice. He gives us a glimpse into the sources upon which he drew most extensively, and into the distillations from those sources which he still values. But he also reveals the reasons why he felt that he had to move on, and sometimes the disillusion and pain that accompanied separation from mentors whom he experienced as constraining his freedoms to pursue other than prescribed pathways.

Readers may find the first part of this book hard going, for the author tries to communicate memories and knowledge now held somewhat globally—much indeed as the infant researchers upon whom he finally draws tell us that babies hold their first 'world knowledge' (Stern 1985). Indeed it is hard to put such comprehensive conglomeration into words; like the infant who tries to translate from the totality of its storehouse of information into words, something is inevitably lost. So we may flounder a bit as Shor attempts to interweave his history and the ideas he gleaned from various experiences.

But clinicians will especially be stimulated by the chapters in which Shor offers in minute detail his approach to patients, even when they may not find it possible to be in entire agreement with some of the principles he advocates. All of his approach is geared toward awarding the patient the agent role in the therapeutic game. He would *negotiate* with the patient all of the details of their working together, rather than prescribing what these should be. He takes a stance *against diagnosis* and even 'diagnostic attitudes' that may be a bit too strong for some of us. I, for example, do not see much value in labels as contributing to our clinical approach. But as a lover of etymology, I would remind us that the word comes from the Greek for 'to distinguish,' and that both patient and therapist have an interest in defining this person as distinct from all others in important ways, these ways contributing to the understanding of his/her complaints. To attempt such knowing is the diagnostic attitude at its best, not just present at the beginning but on-going. We might *play* with the idea that there are two diagnosticians present in clinical interviews, each attempting to understand the other and their interrelationship. As Stern (1985), whom Shor so often quotes, proposes, once the infant has grasped the idea of possible shareable subjectivities, the reach for intersubjectivities becomes a veritable *need*, or at least a fervent wish.

What Shor is most against is the therapist's presuming to know better than the patient what is wrong. So in his approach he does not focus on 'exposing' the possible self-deceptions but rather on creating *safe space* in which the patient may renew capacities for self-exploration and direction. He recommends that we wait for the person's *invitation* before offering any interpretations, and even then they should be offered tentatively, so that the patient may refuse more easily if so inclined. Meanings too must be *negotiated;* the therapist alone cannot arrogate a privileged access to the truth. Although at times he comes close to the position of Personalism, decreeing that the person 'owns' meaning, his approach is ultimately that of Dialogism: *we* own meaning, or "if we do not own it, we may, at least *rent* meaning" (Holquist 1982, p. 3). Or maybe, in this interpersonal approach, we try on for size the meanings offered by the other and sometimes come to claim those we 'borrowed' from the other. Certainly Shor is open to learning from his patients' meanings other than those which his discipline of psychoanalysis might have pronounced.

He would avoid what Stern (1977) calls 'missteps in the dance', those intrusions which can make for a derailing of the dialogue. He believes with Spitz that such derailing may be at the heart of all pathology, and that repair lies in somehow re-railing to facilitate a free exchange of feelings and ideas. Shor sees the patient's prime objective to identify, express, reflect on, and modify feelings. This is very much in keeping with the idea of the self and its 'affective core' (Emde 1983). Especially important to the repair of that sense of core self is the therapist's acknowledging that, while we might be able by listening well and by reading the nonverbal bodily cues to recognize the categorical emotions being manifest, we can never know their quantitative dimensions. As we are reminded by Stern (1985), language is ideal for dealing with the categorical, but it is at a great disadvantage in dealing with gradient information, precisely that which carries the most decisive information for the therapeutic dialogue. So we and our patients are up against some limits of the verbal, no matter how hard we attempt to hone our communicative skills.

Just as Shor does not request the patient to say whatever comes to mind, so he does not *ask* that dreams be brought to him; in fact to do so, he says, will complicate the analysis iatrogenically. Some readers may fear that he assumes an 'archaic stereotypic practice' which may not be true of many analysts of today, and they would affirm that they do attend to the transference considerations in their patients' offering of dream material. I do not suggest that patients share their dream life, for I regard it as the last refuge of the strictly private. But many analysands love their dreams, and find in them particularly that playground of the mind which can be hard to find in waking life. When, in the context of felt attunement with the therapist, they share them, it is a way of *inviting* play, of discovering what of these most private experiences are shareable in ways that can extend both meanings and pleasure.

Shor sees elements of *play* in the making of hypotheses, interpretations, and narratives. But before he can indulge in such play openly with the patient, he must engage in an often extended period of something akin to what Winnicott (1956) called 'primary maternal preoccupation', to the abstinence which the 'clinical infant' (Stern's term) could see as the other having 'no needs or interests of her own'—Balint's description of the terms of 'primary *love.*' So in attunement and in empathy is the love, but also the *work* of containing one's own impulses to intervene prematurely. Work is also done to 'move the patient on beyond empathy' toward the capacity for private play, which clearly means toward the 'capacity to be alone' (Winnicott 1958). Since that, in turn, depends upon a comfortable being alone in the presence of someone, that is what Shor tries to provide.

The author defines that old concept of *resistance* as 'a healthy opposition to impositions.' Perhaps we could hypothesize that some of the opposition of official psychoanalysis to the revisionists and the heretics has been that there is in all of us an identification with the belief systems we have laboriously developed over time, including those inculcated by the specific education and training we have received in our chosen professions. So some of our resistance to change may be healthy too, so long as we are also willing to listen to or read those who would offer alternative ways of viewing things. To some extent, as one of Shor's mentors, Theodor Reik (1951), pointed out, 'heresy is the parent of dogma.' We may anticipate that some colleagues who peruse this book will harden their traditional attitudes. Others, however, may be moved to engage in a dialectic of movement, weighing and measuring for themselves what is of lasting value in the old and what of newer ideas might make for strengthening of theories and practice, and especially for an ethic of practice such as we find in these pages.

My favorite poet, Wallace Stevens (1954) was forever decrying the limits even of poetic language for capturing 'reality.' The best we could do would be to make 'Notes Toward a Supreme Fiction'. Like those inventions of the mind, each production about the psyche ideally meets his three criteria: it must be abstract; it must change; and it must give pleasure. For some of us, Dr. Shor's ideas fulfill these conditions. Certainly they are open-ended and invite our deepening and extending as we work and play with them, maybe even at times overcoming our own resistances to loving them.

References

Stern, D. (1985). *The Interpersonal World of the Infant*. New York: Basic Books.

Holquist, M. (1982). The politics of representation. In S. J. Greenblatt, *Allegory and Representation*. Baltimore, Md.: John Hopkins Press.

Stern, D. (1977). *The First Relationship*. Cambridge, Mass.: Harvard University Press.

Spitz, R. (1963). Life and the dialogue. In *Counterpoint: Libidinal Object and Subject*. Ed. Herbert Gaskill. New York: International Universities Press.

Winnicott, D. W. (1956). Primary maternal preoccupation. In *The Maturational Processes and the Facilitating Environment*. New York: International Universities Press.

Winnicott, D. W. (1958). The capacity to be alone. In *The Maturational Processes and the Facilitating Environment*. New York: International Universities Press.

Reik, T. (1951). *Myth, Dogma and Compulsion*. New York: International Universities Press.

Stevens, W. (1954). Notes toward a supreme fiction. In *Collected Poems of Wallace Stevens*. New York: Alfred A. Knopf.

Jean Sanville

I

Prelude to a Humanist Psychoanalysis

Freud's very first patient report, on Emmy von N., tells the original conception of the psychoanalytic process in 1888. She called for negotiating a safe working relationship, and then expressed her dilemmas and difficult feelings. He offered empathy, "some calming words," and then she invited interpretations. Freud "fell in" with her demands (S.E. II p. 63) and allowed her to be in charge. He recognized learning about the "self-feeling" of the patient (p. 92) as influencing the symptoms, complaints and general mood. He valued Emmy as "admirable . . . her intelligence and energy . . . were no less than a man's and her high degree of education and love of truth . . . her benevolent care for the welfare of all her dependents, her humility of mind and the refinement of her manners revealed her qualities as a true lady as well" (pp. 103–104). Yet she had shown bold resistance to his regular instructions and to his manipulations of her body; but sometimes he suspended his benign authority and yielded to her insistence. Then, she advanced to request his "opinion about all sorts of things that seemed to her important . . . " (p. 63). The psychoanalytic dialogue was born.

This humanist approach reappears at telling moments during the fifty years of Freud's life work but it is only now gaining consistent consideration. Since the 1960's, harmonious observations on dialogues with the newborn infant person are also evoking deep rooted revisions of the orthodox theories and methods. The original sequence of phases, negotiation, empathy and interpretation, will be developed here to give concrete therapeutic meaning to the professional activities of work, love and play. This book is my personal report on these advances beyond the classical attitudes in which I had been trained.

These essays are dedicated to the three psychoanalysts who were most directly influential in my professional development in this field. With each, I worked, loved and played for more than ten years of association and friendship:

with ERNST KRIS (1940–1952)
with THEODOR REIK (1944–1955)
with MICHAEL BALINT (1952–1970)

None might agree, surely not fully, with what I've done with their messages, but I would hope that in ten years neither would I—in the spirit of open-ended dialogue which is the central theme sought here, emerging from an essentially traditional psychoanalysis.

Certain basic values will surely persist and evolve. Expressions of subjectivity can become a fruitful exchange when the ethical relationship develops into a flexible dialogue between persons feeling equally valued. Privacy and confidentiality in the psychotherapeutic experience can protect the reparative patience of the therapist and the patient. However, faulty and abusive practices are generally concealed, whether innocent or exploitative, conscious or unconscious. These essays are mostly about positive and favorable procedures. The unfortunate, negative occurrences are less available for public consideration and correction; for these, the remedies reside in evoking the self-interested alertness and complaining of the patient and in the ethical and personal development of the therapist.

Since that experience of privateness is essential, even if only partially fathomable, the professional therapist can discuss

2

openly only his/her principles of method, aims and ideals. I rely on the protesting patient to guide and improve the effectiveness of our work, love and play together. If the client feels I am failing him, being in charge, he can then choose to leave or to be patient and try again. This is the core of my thesis.

The use of the evaluative term, "ethics," may be troublesome to a traditionally scientific stance, but so also must be the qualities of subjective and private experiencing which are inherent and essential to modern psychotherapy. Now the difficulties for the classical scientist are manifoldly increased as we learn the layers of complexity imbedded in the intersubjectivities of patient and therapist. We need a new respect for the private values which guide the human experience, a greater openness to individual variability and unpredictability. I locate the central ethical issues in the area of our attitudes about human potentialities, our assumptions about their meanings and measures.

My view is that the analytic therapist should, in principle, mainly facilitate the patient's attending to his own hidden values and reflecting on his private ways of making judgments and decisions. The professional helper would aim to avoid all pressuring to persuade the client to any moral position. My assumption, or bias, is that more sensitivity to promote such ethics is possible in practice to assist the client's advances in regaining and developing capacities to move toward his own goals and hopes. In our traditional terms of Superego functions, ethics concern the positive strivings toward Ego Ideals while morality drives through the negative forces of Conscience, the threatening pressures of "No." Ethical values are experienced as "Yes."

Another bias, or preference, in these essays is for more description of the atmosphere and methods in comprehensive detail for clinical practice rather than for the formulation of precise theories. There are helpful cues from recent developments in infant observation and the new attention to intersubjective and empathic aspects of depth psychotherapy; these explorations are involving us in greater speculating about nonverbal exchanges and unverbalized private data. Strict, strong

3

words are too harsh to pronounce on the fluid and evanescent phenomena of multidimensional exchanges, and categorical, diagnostic terms may not capture yet unformulated experiencing; precise verbal distinctions can have a hard, technical impact which constrains and constricts the subject matter, much as do moralistic dicta, in my view. Such severity imposes a note of crisis; the result may be a limiting of alternatives and possibilities for further development, a discouraging of new discoveries or creations. Definitive formulation may suggest an urgent need for active measures to prevent anticipated disasters, a time when exploratory psychotherapy is not to be risked. Play and patience suffer for both patient and therapist.

Yet we know a certain security can be felt when a neat system of categories and differentiations provides a promise of safe space; then, holding the terms loosely, we can look about more freely for variations and exceptions to the imposing frame and sets. Used this way a scheme of ideas can serve fruitfully. We each have our paces of alternating safety and freedom so that the oscillation may become a growing spiral which soon shapes a next turn in a dialectic. The shifts in language will signify the enriched meanings.

An early example comes to mind. As a sophomore, when psychology was within the philosophy department, I was very much moved by a formulation about a sequence of basic human wishes, "subjective purposes," found by Thomas and Znaniecki, in *The Polish Peasant* (1918): *security, recognition, response* and *new experience*. These old words may be redefined to be richly relevant ideas seventy years later; now *safe space, projective identity, intersubjective exchange* and *play* carry the current implications for social policy and for psychotherapy. The newer meanings will be found in the modified methods of practice which are arising from below, the freed-up awareness in our culture.

My present emphasis on the experiencing of analytic psychotherapy assumes some suspension of exact theoretical and diagnostic formulations in the hope of liberating additional data. Yet, I do propose a broad set of hypotheses about basic drives based on Freud's original (1905) instinct theory (source,

4

aim and object) and I immediately apply these abstractions to concrete clinical details of practice under the primacy of subjective and ethical considerations.

Since 1972, Jean Sanville has been the most significant influence in my further development and this alliance continues. Our joint and separate presentations (see References) suggest some of that interplay in their overlapping foci and differing styles. We concluded our 1978 book (Shor and Sanville, p. 140) with this program:

> Freud's advice for the good life, that one aims to achieve satisfaction from love and work (SE XXI pp. 80–94), may now be expanded. We speak for including the qualities of playfulness and for allowing them to permeate loving and working. Thus we hope to reach the love in work and in play; to enjoy the work in love and in play; and most deeply, to explore the play in working and loving.

II

Some Ethical Assumptions

In 1970 I was meeting again with Michael Balint in London to discuss our joint interests and make plans to further a line of clinical thinking which had emerged for me in reading his *Primary Love and Psychoanalytic Technique* in 1952, when our correspondence began. We had maintained continuous exchanges over the years and he had helped to arrange for my three years nearbye, on staff of Tavistock Clinic and a guest membership in the British Psycho-Analytic Society, in the early 1960s. In those years I learned at close hand much more about the thinking and attitudes of many of the British independent analysts, including Balint. I also participated in providing psychoanalytic therapy for physicians in the Balint Doctor's Group but we were clear that there were special challenges in his more deeply psychoanalytic ideas about a primary positive sense of personhood within the earliest infant experiences.

This promising perspective for human growth and repair is the ethical springboard for the personal-professional ideas and narratives in these essays. Balint's speculations about that aliveness, as a prelude to creative entitlement beyond mere bliss and survival, first appeared in a 1932 publication on benign regression and the new beginning experience in therapy, building on Ferenczi's earlier (1908) work on reparative intentions rooted in primary object love. This clinical theme about original resources for self repair engaged me very particularly and I became puzzled about the decades of general neglect of it by colleagues. Yet, Balint was elected President of the British Society in 1969, an act of being elevated instead of being offered dialogue, as I saw it. After my essay review (1969) of his *The Basic Fault*, he had invited me to join him in a further developing of our now common perspective.

My move to London in 1970 was made with much excitement and enthusiasm, having found my way through an orthodox, classical training influenced mostly by Ernst Kris and Theodor Reik from 1946 to 1952, and then through some explorations of several divergent schools in New York City. The meetings with Balint were developing well in mid-1970 but his health began to fail that Fall and he died soon after Christmas. During our last conversations, I suggested a fresh focus on the increasing phenomena of repeat analyses, which I had termed "experienced patients" in a 1963 article on Darwin and Freud.

Analytic review of that jointly reflective data might be a rich source for new theory and method. Also, since the 1960s there have been new observations on infants, especially by Spitz (1963), which described early pre-verbal states of quiet alert and of non-verbal negotiation and dialogue processes. In a joint book, *Illusion in Loving* (1978), Shor and Sanville develop the theme that such primary positive experiences are models for and motivations in all psychotherapy. The present essays are my attempt to shape these several lines of thought to modify clinical theory and practice.

This is also a narrative about a humanist perspective in psychotherapy and an accounting of difficulties and advances in my professional development from orthodoxy towards the open-ended values I now see as central to psychoanalytic practice. I was engaged early with Freud's writings and began working towards a career as psychoanalyst in 1935. The reports of personal experiences are accompanied with some edited se-

7

lections from my own unpublished writings en route to my current mosaic of ideas, concepts and ethical considerations.

The long journey is reconstructed to reach for some integrations of major trends among colleagues' concerns and controversies; the whole work is an effort for "integrity in the eighth stage" (Erikson, *Identity and the Life Cycle,* 1959). One hopes to avoid polemics as well as confessional or boasting tones, though my basic thesis about the permeating qualities of complaining and repairing in the human condition makes such abstinence difficult. It may help if, at once, I call on another crucial notion in my present approach, the intrinsic role of playfulness in the human experience.

I understand play not as a marginal epiphenomenon but as inherent in human evolution, neurally rooted, within the multidimensionality which creates the actuality of experiencing. A most expansive and playful statement of this opening approach is given in R. Fischer's article, "On fact and fiction—the structure of stories that the brain tells to itself about itself," which takes us "beyond good and evil" (1987, p. 350). Play includes a capacity for a flexible neutrality. While the humanist psychotherapist will respect the urgencies presented by the patient and meet them with sensitive empathies, we need not internalize the anxieties as our own or take charge in defense.

If we allow that playing with theories about psychotherapy may relieve the hidden private investments and agenda of the professional practitioner, we might free up the actual relating between patient and doctor. One is reminded of Freud's critical comments about therapists driven by a *"furor sanandi"* to replace their traditional *furor diagnosticus* (in S. Ferenczi's *Clinical Diary* 1933). If we do less earnest caring for and less sympathizing, we may offer better care, more flexible negotiation, richer empathy, more useful love.

We work with persons presenting pain and discontent, and our conscientious efforts come with powerful, often hidden, assumptions and presumptions about our clients' limitations and potentialities. In the conventional tradition, we have served as benign, responsible resources but we supported ourselves in this complex work by holding ourselves as authorities

8

for unfortunate sufferers. We have remained in charge of the psychotherapeutic process despite Freud's frequent advices for a contrary position:

> It is left to the patient in all essentials to determine the course of the analysis and the arrangement of the material; any systematic handling of particular symptoms or complexes thus becomes impossible. (S.E. XX, p. 41)

> I allow each patient to break off whenever he likes. (S.E. XII, p. 129)

> After all, analysis does not set out to make pathological reactions impossible, but to give the patient's ego freedom to decide one way or the other. (S.E. XIX, p. 50)

And Freud left us this challenge to be open to irregular and unpredictable data, beyond the cohesive rationality of ego psychology, in his last, unfinished, paper, normalizing "the splitting of the Ego":

> I find myself for a moment in the interesting position of not knowing whether what I have to say should be regarded as something long familiar and obvious or as something essentially new and puzzling. But I am inclined to think the latter. . . . We take for granted the synthetic nature of the processes of the ego. But we are clearly at fault in this. The synthetic function . . . is subject to particular conditions and is liable to a whole number of disturbances. (S.E. XXIII, pp. 275–6)

And, much earlier, in 1914, he described his basic method, his "technique":

> The main instrument . . . consists in the handling of the transference . . . (as) a playground, in which it is allowed to let itself go in almost complete freedom. . . . The doctor has nothing else to do than to wait and let things take their course, a course which cannot be avoided nor always hastened. (S.E. XII, pp. 149–155)

His final instructions, about terminating treatment, recommend modesty:

9

Here it is not easy to predict a natural end to the process. . . . The business of analysis is to secure the best possible conditions for the functioning of the ego; when this has been done, analysis has accomplished its task. (S.E. XXXIII, p. 250)

Such advice to be patient and modest in our experiencing the patient experiencing has, in my view, begun to take root and has yielded fruit most fully in the developments of the British tradition of Independent analysts (Kohon, 1986). Their influence, especially from Balint and Winnicott, will be very evident in these essays, particularly their respect for self-pacing and playfulness, in principle if not in systematic detail.

These horizons have stimulated our work, together and separately to this date. Jean Sanville has written a comprehensive analysis of *The Play in Clinical Education* (1979) and several other developments of these ideas (1979a, 1982, 1987). We each begin with the recognition of playful capacities and responsive sensitivities in the early infant as cues for our hypotheses about the therapeutic potentialities for advancing dialogue processes in the details of clinical practice. My recent review of Spitz's life work, *Dialogues from Infancy* (Shor, 1985), begins to note starts in American psychoanalysis in this direction; others will be identified in subsequent chapters.

Of course I am selecting my "Freud" to support my views; so rich a source is his life work. Freshly trained in the classical model, I was exercising the orthodox ways until, in 1952, I read young Balint's bold critique (1932) of his teacher, Ferenczi, on a principle of method which I see as a cardinal consideration in the ethics of self pacing in the therapeutic relationship and which is at the core of my approach now:

That is the crucial point: *that the amount of excitation, the degree of the tension is actually determined by the patient himself.* This explains why in many cases the otherwise useful interventions (such as those recommended by Ferenczi) . . . remain ineffectual. Accordingly one tried to let the patient determine himself the amount of tension or excitement he could bear. . . . Doubtless patient waiting and interpreting is the surest and, in most cases, the most effecacious method. (1932, in *Primary Love*, 1952, pp. 155–156; italics in original text).

Central to these essays is a set of hypotheses about the basic complaints and desires which may underlie all patients' tensions and discontents, and a therapeutic approach which does not interpret until invited. Whatever symptoms or diagnostic indications are presented, the patient is met with flexible negotiations and then with graded empathies; when these efforts develop a working alliance which confirms the client's sense of active leadership, he will choose to call on the therapist for possible meanings to be considered together or separately.

This programme is rooted in an attempt to bridge that "ever widening gap" (Freud, 1938, p. 275) between the mastery of reality and the fulfillment of fantasy, "both of which are valid and effective . . . and this success is achieved at the price of a rift in the ego which never heals but which increases as time goes on" (ibid); he allows for a normal and inevitable "splitting in the ego" (ibid) which challenges the whole tradition of ego synthesis.

I think this fresh idea has provoked some major trends in American psychoanalysis: the revolts against energy concepts, drive theory and all metapsychology; the controversies between self psychology and object relations theories; and the very recent emphases on empathy and intersubjectivities. Many other resolutions are proposed in Grolnick's *Between Reality and Fantasy* (1978). Some theoreticians have turned to systems and information theories to encompass or cover the space between fantasy and reality.

I'm returning to Freud's first formulations about "instinct" theory (1905) to suggest that his prime terms, *source, aim* and *object*, always imply particular aspects of both a self and a relationship. Their core qualities may be translated into the patient's private expressions of complaints and desires: feeling *supplied* with valued vital energies and resources, feeling safe and free to become *expressive* with skill and pleasure, and feeling met by responsive others ready to *exchange*. To phrase our

11

empathies and interpretations in such experience-near terminology may keep us closer to the person's hidden suffering and
hopes for both self and relationships. If we attend to and identify the basic reparative intentions in the person, we are respecting the humanistic ethic of psychotherapy, and of
developmental care, which pervades this approach to the human condition. Such focus on subjective discontent may guide
us to develop a more intrinsic framework of psychological motivations. Freud remained dissatisfied with his speculations:
"There is no more urgent need in psychology than for a se-
curely founded theory of the instincts. . . . " (S.E. XX p. 56).

The impetus to growth, maturation, development and to
psycho-therapy may be seen to be nourished by the impulses
to complain, to distrust, to compromise and then to complain
further on another level. Complaining can be led to evoke and
be a prod to a consciousness which focusses attention and effort for a repair, internally and externally. The new adaptations, revisions and discoveries are advantageous for natural
selection and evolution. With creative solutions, there emerges
a dialectical spiral fueled by some inherent models for being
and becoming. But even successful adjustments run out and
stimulate new claims and clamors for fuller, higher satisfactions. Private reflecting is never done. When one calls on
help, the assistance must try to remain open to unpredictable
forms of complaints and desires. The helper's task is first to
maintain a readiness to hear hidden and unconscious cues and
to develop an atmosphere and relationship with patients such
that they invite our hypotheses and interpretations. Let me
sketch the programme to be developed.

My largest hypothesis is that the therapist's activity and
presence can best meet patient complaints and desires if he
offers certain forms of *work, love* and *play;* the patient can
best define and refine the pace and the measures of his pains
and satisfaction in his capacities for experiencing work, love
and play. The client's estimates are subject to error and illusion
but his self reparative wishes will make the corrections he feels
necessary. The therapist offers an individualized sequence of

12

responsive dialogue processes: interweaving negotiations, empathy and transference interpretations.

No advance life history or diagnostic formulation is necessary—and in fact may well be obstructive, producing iatrogenic resistances. I see confrontation and "resistance" analysis as harmful to the therapeutic alliance; they obstruct the deepest affective outcomes. These keynotes are at the heart of my thesis.

My earliest assumptions are that all pathologies are privately and subjectively defined variants of felt *deprivation*, *suppression* and *frustration* (Shor, 1963). Each developmental failure of resonance, every dissonance, violates a primary wish and provokes a defense which may take a pathogenic turn; these traumatic experiences are behind all discontents, about self esteem, status, power or fulfillment. Therapy will aim to help unwind the painful twist in the hidden complaint if the sufferer is allowed to guide the process through benign reparative regressions (Shor, 1972). The patient's active attitude frees energies and hopes to renew and redo his efforts. He can best select and measure good enough experiences about resources, about skilled functioning with pleasure and about exchanging, sharing, merging and separating. The client will determine the pace of our sessions and the terminations.

The friendly humanistic atmosphere of patient, refined negotiating and empathizing will free the client to find his way through the defensive structures and transference distortions and to use our tentative interpretations and our modest suggestions, when invited. Our humble cooperation will allow a fuller listening to the patient's petitions and responsiveness (Freud, S.E. XXIII pp. 257–269) and a richer learning as he/she guides and teaches us (Casement, 1985). We take private responsibilities for our professional role playing, our personal readiness and the countertransferences which may obstruct our open patience. Instead of filling that "ever widening gap," (Freud, 1938) we may equip ourselves to better learn with each person to create and play in the ever transitional space (Winnicott, 1971) which contains psychic reality.

13

If we may think of ourselves, all of us, as experienced patients, suffering some inevitable and contingent deprivations, suppressions and frustrations, a note of complaint and a reach for repair may well permeate the human condition. Although noises of primary discontent and desire can disturb everyone, there are usually caretakers who come to listen to meet demands of the new-born and to satisfy enough needs and potentialities for survival. As personal and cultural developments occur, the plaintive and joyful sounds are elaborated symbolically and the search for forms of fulfillment seems to increase in sensitiveness and variety. Beyond the goals of survival and satisfaction, there emerge new ideas of striving for "perfection", but the images are elusive, highly subjective, private and changing.

Wider aims may also appear even at birth in "quiet alert states" (Wolff, 1959) and then reach to experience novelty, creativeness and wonder (Milner, M., 1937, 1950, 1969, 1987; Pierce, C. S., 1923; Fiske, P. W. and Maddi, S. R., 1961). Greenacre has described the early infant's positive use of experiences of awe, in her *Emotional Growth* (1956 and 1959). Whatever the sources of discontent, deficiency, damage, conflict or hopes for unrealized potentialities, some measures and forms of psychotherapy appear in every society (Shor, 1948). Such caretaking activity may complement human neural openness and both processes may evolve best from inherent capacities for dialogue or exchange.

My early professional training, from about 1935 to 1952, was within the benign authoritarian tradition, with its careful diagnoses and criteria of cure. Moved especially by Balint's 1952 book on *Primary Love*, a new era began to develop for me. My recent decades are more concerned first with the interplay between the two persons, plaintiff and protective resource. I've come to offer clear priority to negotiation, to empathy, to intersubjectivity, and to developing dialogue in a felt safe interaction, and with constant attention to and respect for the variable private experience.

The presented complaints and desires are changing in a dialectical series of cultural revolutions about individual choice and self fulfillment for minorities now claiming equal civil rights; we see a flourishing of rising expectations. The practices in psychotherapies are actually loosening among some clinicians and healers but a stereotypical model of classical orthodox method continues to haunt, as a burden and disadvantage, I feel. Michael Balint has dared, yet sensitively (1952, 1959, 1968), to suggest principled considerations towards basic modifications in our methods; and some American writers have made steps in these directions: e.g. A. Goldberg (1987) and A. Lazare (1975, 1988) on negotiation, M. Gill (1982, 1988) and S. Leavy (1980) on dialogue, and L. Havens on empathy (1986). The trends to more flexible attitudes about therapy practices are gaining cultural and conceptual stimuli as well as special support from the new infant observations which are boldly speculative and also open to the same issues of unverbalized subjectivities and projections of private ethics.

Thus, effective "trauma" are not easily defined objectively; the continuities between bad experiences in early personal development and later problems are not simply parallel processes. Because of the private subjectivities (Freud, SE XX p. 106) we have to learn with each person what persists and what is modified by inner resources or later experiences. Yet, if in some aspects each of us is indeed an experienced patient, those qualities of complaint and hopes for reparation will create both continuing conflicts and anchoring bonds. There are always some felt breaks between fantasy and reality, between anticipation and actuality, whether in common or uniquely. We were alerted to this "ever widening gap" in Freud's final but unfinished clinical message (1938) about "the split in the ego" with the inherent "series of disturbances."

Present enthusiasms for "the cohesive self" (Kohut, 1976) and for the goal of successful relating (Kernberg, 1978) may be seen as illusions, both necessary for ongoing development; they may be combined into a model of open-ended evolution, an oscillating spiral in a flexible dialogue (Shor and Sanville, 1978). Recent advances in infant observations and theory (Spitz, 1984, Hack, 1975, Stern, 1985, Blatt, 1986, Trevarthan, 1982, 1987, et. al.) all serve to support this effort to reform the

15

shape of psychotherapeutic events into a medley of special dialogue processes: negotiation, empathy, interpretation and an ever increasing respect for the patient's autonomy.

Open ended evolution has become a leading perspective in Western culture, propelled further by the work of both Darwin and Freud. Darwin, as "grandfather of modern psychotherapy" (Shor, 1963 p. 11) especially identified the role of empathy, extending and expanding man's social instincts and sympathies with increasing regard for: "not only the welfare but the happiness of his fellow men . . . his sympathies became more tender and widely diffused, extending to men of all races, to the imbecile, maimed, and other useless members of society, and finally to the lower animals,—so would the standard of his morality rise higher and higher." (1871, p. 493). Darwin's thesis for broadening empathies suggests the capacity for benign regression as progression evolves. Balint links this theme to his special contributions in advancing the daring ideal of "Progression for the sake of Regression" (1959, chapter X).

The subsequent emergence of psychoanalytic thinking continues to implement this expansion despite the ever new social complications and professional controversies. Current challenges to old orthodoxies, with their diagnostic attitudes, are producing new flexibilities in our theories and methods for psychotherapy, enriched by recent decades of broad public complaint and bold private experimentation (Shor, 1970). Our society with its tradition for an individualistic ethic has liberated a self-assertive exploration of human possibilities, which yields cues to professional psychotherapists.

Alongside the cultural values of individualism there is emerging a balancing recognition of the significance of exchange and dialogue, even at the highest levels of legal authority. The U.S. Supreme Court, as the start of a generation of civil rights advances and functioning as a progressive analyst, "as a partner in a dialogue" (Stone, C.D. 1971), decided in 1954 (Brown vs. Board of Education) that "separate but equal" experience is not good enough for full human development;

16

interaction and dialogue are now seen as necessary towards the psychic unity of all humanity.

Both dimensions of this dialectic spiral, this double helix of autonomy and intimacy (Shor and Sanville, 1978) are core personal values to be given equal attention, for the further progress of psychotherapy as well. This thesis on ethics is explored here in the details of clinical practice to further the freeing of dialogue, beyond concern with survival and beyond classical methods in psychotherapy.

Since the assumptions hidden in the therapist's attitudes may be the most difficult obstacles to furthering dialogue, I will try to share relevant details of my professional development. The pervading clinical challenge is to be available with possibly helpful hypotheses while respecting the principle that the patient remains basically in charge. Marion Milner, a prominent member of the British Independents, puts this perspective as follows:

> What heals my patients? Not me. I only try to clear away the blocks so that they can find the discovering activity in themselves, the inner grace. And have the grace to recognize it (1987, p. 103).

I see this aim of liberating the self liberating potentialities as essentially equivalent to the more traditional terms: "The analyst is . . . a facilitator of the capacity to become a self-analyst" (Rangell, 1988, p. 336). In 1908, Ferenczi, Balint's major teacher, put it most profoundly: "We are only fitted for our task when we endeavor to assist, so far as in us lies, the diseased organism's attempts at self cure" (1926, p. 26). Today we are only beginning to develop its advancing clinical implications.

Pronouncing ethical principles is much too easy and indulgent, and not difficult to abstract away or evade. Since we are all experienced patients to some degree, one is generically distrustful of, or submissive to another's high minded formulations. Each of us has the task of testing new notions in the

17

details of private experiencing, as therapist and as patient. Then we can develop our specific and flexible ways of work, love and play which may fulfill our unique sources, aims and objects.

The fine line between individual uniqueness and a core of common meanings in human experiencing is a shifting border, sometimes fuzzy and often open to confusion, conflict or cooperation. We strain to manage the unpredictability of responses to our reaching for flexible dialogue. I remember a celebration of women's liberation towards more equal exchange (Shor, 1954) which applied Balint's (1932) pronouncement of benign regression and new beginnings; his promise for freeing hidden potentialities is still not appreciated, I feel. My article then distanced many close colleagues and provoked an independent, sometimes defiant, search for fresh sources, aims and objects in my professional, and personal, developments. The ongoing correspondence with Balint yielded enough safe space for further explorations. I questioned classical theories and methods to pursue my personal values for dialogue processes in depth psychotherapy. His early death has accelerated my efforts.

III

From Subjectivity to Professional Responsibility

Most psychotherapists today are likely to have some experienced patients, who previously had consulted other therapists and left unsatisfied. Their reports of "failure" are complex selective messages of discontent and hope, mixing old and new complaints and desires. Their narratives may include memories of successful moments which were lost and also teasing visions which moved them to fresh efforts. These are rich data that could illuminate both the variable approaches to treatment and the unrecognized individual pathways to unforeseen satisfying change; but, since we cannot repeat such natural experiments with classically rigorous, scientific procedures, the complicated motivations in these accounts and in their interpretations render the data into unresolvable controversy, polemics, rumor, gossip and neglect.

Yet, each of us in practice can come to know best his own changes of approach to patients over the years, even with the same patient, as he or we advance in insight and maturity, and, being closest to the private processes, each of us can best make hypotheses about the clinical experience and new approaches as perceived freshly within ourselves. The subjectivity can thus be enriched and permit a fuller abstraction of principles and more sensitive generalizations, which may engage the interests of others in their practice with patients or in themselves.

Psychiatry in the century before Freud emphasized diagnostic labelling, usually with fixed innate differentiations. Yet today a necessary assumption for any useful knowledge and empathy in general psychology and in psychotherapy is some approximation, however delicate and careful, to the idea of a qualitative psychic unity of human potentialities, at least at the beginning of life. This universalizing and humanizing idea is gaining suggestive support from the recent observational data and tentative formulations about the global and cross-dimensional qualities in the first appearances of a self, in the neonate (Blatt, 1987 and Trevarthan, 1984). Darwin had begun to gather the data in his late studies of emotional expression (1872). His evolutionary perspective has decreased diagnostic attitudes.

The hope for a science of private experience has lurked uneasily in the deep shadows of psychoanalysis for over a century. Freud proclaimed this aim in his first decade but soon withdrew his "Project for a Scientific Psychology" before any publication. The effort to renew that original project has been revived several times, in attempts at new metapsychology, but each time many fellow clinicians showed mostly rejection or neglect. In more recent decades, leading analysts have attacked Freud's concepts of "drive" "instinct," "energy" and all other metapsychological formulations modeled on the physical sciences. Most protestors named such abstractions as irrelevant or distorting to the clinical practice with experiencing patients.

Within ten years of Freud's abandonment of his 1895 "Project," he had advanced systematic hypotheses about dreams, slips, memory, humor and specific syndromes in personal development, and to this day these theories nourish and also embattle many fields of social studies, art, history, linguistics, literature, sociology and much more. The "natural" and physical sciences have mostly attacked or ignored psychoanalytic metapsychology, and now neuroscience and information theory make ambitious projects to finally fathom depth psychology with their own concepts.

Psychopharmocologists evoke great excitement in professionals and patients about chemical controls of the psyche; at their best, these researchers may consult the subjects on side effects and there are beginnings of a partnership relationship to refine the technical measures. Some express the larger hope to become free eventually of the need to submit to physical agents but anxious, dependent patients often collude to extend the era of chemical intrusions despite the dulling and controlling effects.

Meanwhile neuroscience searches for further basic hypotheses. Perhaps this phase of gathering the subjective data in a developing partnership with the experiencer will narrow the gap in comprehension and permit a friendlier interaction between the scientific and humanistic forces in the human condition. Some neurologists, like K. Pribram (1971), have renewed adventurous consideration of Freud's first hypotheses for laboratory investigation. The tension between science and clinical practice has begun to produce a fruitful dialogue. The Journal of the American Medical Association advises that "self-awareness is the key to utilizing these [emotional] reactions to improve the patient-physician relationship" in an article entitled "Doctors have Feelings Too" (Zinn, p. 3296); here, medical measures may blur emotions which influence psyche and soma. Yet Freud saw medical training as a sometimes curable obstacle to good psychoanalytic work (S.E. XX, pp. 251–258).

What may be promising is the sensitive refining of the doctor-patient partnership to encompass more of the private, personal, subjective experiencing of both persons. It can begin to approach the model of an evolving dialogue with less of the traditional professional condescension and manipulation. A new respectful image of the person is emerging in the findings of many current observers of early human development; a pioneer here, R. Spitz, closed his decades of research with "unexpected findings" in *Dialogue from Infancy* (1985). How can

21

both the therapist and the observer allow for major surprises and unpredictabilities implicit in the new regard for the private person?

Among the clinical psychoanalysts, an "Independent" tradition (G. Kohon, 1986) has been identified in the work of M. Balint, D. W. Winnicott, M. Milner, et al., as far back as the 1930s with fresh attention to the privacy rights and latent creative potentialities of every patient, whatever may have been the official diagnoses pronounced. The consolidating idea behind all these trends is, in my view, the sensitive searching by therapist and patient for the sometime hidden wishes for both self-paced autonomy and for exchange as equally primary in each person (Shor and Sanville, 1978). Thus, the ethics of the therapeutic relationship may come into focus, and the clinical partnership move to become a special kind of dialogue.

No longer must we resign ourselves to the manipulations or "conditionings", implied in the "black box" concept of the behavioristic psychologists; nor need we fear the vanishing of realistic insight and illumination because of awesome cosmic threats, from astronomers, physicists or spiritualists, of the "black hole" vortex which suspends all awareness of the sense of self. Yet, both images, mechanistic and transcendental, may be moments occurring within the expanding range of normal human experiencing and may enrich and extend the space and pace of experiencing selfhood. Zinberg has richly explored potential flexibilities for *Alternate States of Consciousness* (1977).

There can be no final body of data for a science of psychology. The complaints and desires in living continue to change as society evolves and as it contrives to meet the discontents and the aims it engenders. Scientific and popular psychotherapy have a long history of doctrines and technical procedures (Shor, 1948), now with many new professions and cults emerging to exercise and rationalize each new dogma or formulation. Schools and institutes have proliferated and contend for social and legal respectability, employing many nearly equivalent concepts. Though the names "psychoanalysis," "unconscious," "ego," "libido," et al. are in wide disfavor, even among psychoanalytically trained therapists, the essential dynamic analytic concepts do become part of our sociology of knowledge (Kris, Herma and Shor, 1943). Each generation and every group seeks to shape its identity and demands its own terms for making advances over older ideas.

As professionals stretch to respond to patients' and public protests, it becomes more difficult to distinguish between some "official" psychotherapies and other sources for healing and mental health; and the potential patient seems less rigid about making a distinction. Old professional establishments are failing to stop the extension of licensure, certification and tolerance to new groups of therapists, counsellors and consultants. Each of these new professions claims a separate and unique identity and may advance its own formulations and treatments. Clients feel a greater choice and often try a variety of approaches in a spirit of flexibility and autonomy. The rejection of role-playing authorities is even more evident in the mushrooming of peer and self-help groups without direct supervision by professional experts. Psychotherapy is increasingly a self-regulating democratic experience, perhaps reflecting the growing culture of civil rights. Do we need a Bill of Rights for patients?

The professional helper may redefine his role and refine functioning in this changing social atmosphere. Though most traditional psychotherapists maintain benignly intrusive measures, formulating case histories, manipulating drug therapies, imposing testing instruments or declaring technical diagnoses, a few are allowing the client to lead the way while they learn to listen and listen to learn. A new note of genuine humility appears as we hear more about negotiation, empathy, dialogue and respect for the pace of the patient. Our culture has been absorbing the ideas of psychodynamic psychotherapy for several decades (Kris, Herma and Shor, 1943). Bold theoreticians have begun further advances to new theories of development, but they remain hesitant about revising the methods of their clinical practice (Shor, 1985). Complex countertransferences are considerations here.

The delicate dialectic between theory and practice is surely inherent in human evolution and each researcher traces a personal path moved by private subjective motives. Although these may never be fully known to oneself or to others, the effort to articulate links and phases may be useful for a next step of discovering what may yet be possible. My self-reporting may be more informative than careful academic discussions of original texts or lengthy case accounts. I do neither here, on principle; no long case reports or extended metapsychology are given. Protracted abstractions or selective narratives of multi-level dynamics blur basic processes; brief illustrations of essential ideas are more suggestive, in my view. My presumption may earn some tolerance if the private details about inner experience as a therapist yield new cues to neglected considerations and to suggestive hypotheses for further refinement. This personal journey is not yet finished but some maps are laid out, some sites marked and many risks recognized.

That rich heritage of theory, from Freud through to the current pioneers, is adopted selectively; so also is the clinical experience sifted to support hidden assumptions and anticipations. I am concerned whether and in what specific ways psychotherapy will remain a professional specialization to be respected as an authoritative expertise. There have always been many pre-scientific cultural traditions of official helpers (Shor, 1948); these continue and flourish today in forms improved by the stimulus of psychodynamic theories. This subtle dialectic evolves in the shadows of social and individual efforts at self correction and recognitions of previously unforeseen difficulties. The patient only can be nearest to the essential, privately subjective data: the layers and links in motivations, the measures of pains, hopes and pleasures and the ultimate judgments about satisfactory experiencing. We cannot presume to know the basic qualities and quantities of the patient's private data better than the subject can.

Such personal values are rooted in the humanistic ethic implicit in our work. The professional task has been to give up some of the trained role playing in psychotherapy as a technical manager of helpless subjects. I now try to offer myself as an auxiliary, hired observer ready to be invited to explore tentative hypotheses while the client remains in charge. Only I can take responsibility for those personal vulnerabilities which cause the intrusions, the neglects and other indications of inner obstacles to sensitive empathies, to approximate interpretations and to tact (Reik, 1937). The goal is to offer and facilitate a deepening respect for the unique pace and unpredictable possibilities of each person. Selected aspects of my personal-professional history have helped to develop my appreciation of the complexities in this approach in actual practice. Some early teachers facilitated my change; others discouraged it.

In the discussion period for the "Panel on the Use of the Economic Viewpoint in Clinical Psychoanalysis" during the 1969 International Psychoanalytic Congress, I suggested that "the chief work of the analyst is to create an atmosphere in which the patient feels free to focus on his inner self (and) use his own psychic forces," powers and resources which were being projected around the therapist. I said then that we use transference interpretations to give the capacity for his desired potentialities back to the patient. I proposed that from the first contact we should negotiate explicitly about all arrangements and procedures, whenever we sense fixed, rigid assumptions in the patient, "whatever the diagnostic indications may be" (*Int. J. Psa.* V. 51, p. 247). This approach was summarily put aside as "just too simplistic" by a panel member (R. Loewenstein) who had been one of my teachers during my years of orthodox classical training twenty years prior to this occasion. I then began to recognize the challenge of developing my point of view more comprehensively.

A theoretical framework was needed to contain the loose set of attitudes I was proposing. I had made some starts in a 1963 article: "Listening to the more experienced complaining of these [experienced] patients with longer delays before interpreting, I came to differentiate three types of traumata: deprivation (source), suppression (aim) and frustration (object)." And in 1972, Loewenstein rejoined me by his suggestion that "it was unfortunate that Freud relinquished the very valuable concepts of impetus, source, aim and object" (*Int. J. Psychoan.*

V. 53, p. 16). These terms have become the backbone for both the clinical and ethical developments to be described here.

But there were earlier stimuli to my perspective. R. Spitz, another of my instructors from the years at the New York Psychoanalytic Institute, had long established the theme of maternal deprivation and the evidences for infant smiling as a social exchange in the first months of life. In 1962 he announced "an unexpected finding," beyond both traditional emphases on ego psychology and object relations theory. He proceeded to describe a variable oscillation between concern with the self and concern with the other; he offered a celebration of "Life and the Dialogue" in 1963. Yet he never applied this idea from infant observations to adult clinical psychotherapy.

I remembered Ferenczi's use of the "oscillation" idea (1913) to extend Freud's first views on development but his experiments with clinical method had run into difficulties (Balint, 1932). The current failure to link theory with method is examined in a recent review of mine (Shor, 1985) where the practical challenge is identified; but these professional ideas also had profound personal sources, of course.

A most powerful memory from childhood was the firm family tradition of Friday evening seminar discussions at the dining table. It was fostered by my father to encourage a spirit of dialogue among us, five children ranging up into late adolescence. Each child, from age five on, was given center stage to express opinions and questions about any theme, from the personal, familial, social, political, scientific, or abstract, ethical realm, all manner of complaints and desires. The core idea of open exploratory discussion to evoke hidden issues and conflicts in a prescribed safe space has persisted for me as a model for the most valued human relationships including psychotherapy. And I've come to assume that this image of relating in free and equal dialogue in safety is a primary and ultimate hope of the patients I meet in professional practice, whatever may be the complaints and ambitions first presented.

It was the qualities of exchange and sharing in Freud's style in his *General Introduction to Psychoanalysis* (1917) which anchored my decision at sixteen to become a psychoanalyst eventually. I began a four-year training experience in clinical psychology at the Clinic of the City University of New York, starting in 1935. In 1939, I was appointed to a full-time position as staff therapist. I met Ernst Kris in 1940 at the Graduate Faculty of the New School for Social Research; at that time this refuge for European émigres offered the opportunity to study with K. Horney, E. Fromm, W. Reich and many other leaders from the psychological and social sciences. Controversy was flagrant; the founder of the Gestalt School, M. Wertheimer, declared: "Psychoanalysis is peripheral to psychology proper." I chose Kris and for twelve years I enjoyed functioning as his student, teaching assistant, research assistant, co-author and friend.

Following four years (1942–46) as a clinical psychologist in the U.S. Army Neuropsychiatric Training Centers, I was accepted as a candidate at the New York Psychoanalytic Institute, in 1946. When the psychiatric and psychoanalytic establishments suspended non-medical candidates, in 1948, I left to help develop a broader Institute under Theodor Reik, from 1948 to 1955. When this new group later discouraged an open research attitude to our field, I examined the ideas of alternative groups in New York and in England. The style and ethic of Michael Balint's responsiveness in our correspondence from 1952 on was the most inviting. His highly original *Thrills and Regressions* in 1959 moved me to England and three years as Research Associate and Faculty at the Tavistock Clinic, as well as a guest member in the British Psycho-analytic Society. In 1964, I returned to the United States, this time to Los Angeles, that frontier of Western civilization, where I sensed new human data was evolving.

The California medical societies, however, were also formally opposed to non-medical psychoanalysis, though I was invited to participate in their basic research for five years. So, several of us began in 1968 to develop a new Los Angeles Institute, which, however, also continues in an essentially classical format, wary of questioning orthodox models and methods, so far.

What makes for such firm and frequent doctrinal hardening of the exploratory spirit in the psychoanalytic Institutes, even in those programs born out of protest, innovation and defiance? Is the need for feeling a safe space especially strong when we practice with problems of unconscious dynamics? Are these recurrent restrictions expressive of certain professional difficulties with the inherently unverifiable nature of hidden psychological forces? These dilemmas seem to haunt the movements in psychotherapy.

My focus here is on "the inner experience of the psychoanalyst" (Reik, 1937) and the style of expression and communication in the relationship of psychotherapy. You will surely remind me that the manners in such exchanges are products of the hidden ethics of the professional and the basic role-playing assumptions of the patient and the therapist about one another. These problems are approachable, if not fully solvable.

My primary preoccupation for five decades with the theories and practices of psychoanalysis may be a peculiar concentration of interest, subject to personal projections of values and biases. Increasingly, many colleagues, experienced practitioners, are publishing their summary perspective as our field completes a century of public presence. The new generations of clinicians seem less bound by strict formulations or by previous dogmas and doctrines. The fresh variety of pronouncements may be found to imply more common assumptions about human development and change.

Even the recent era of confrontation and divisiveness between self psychology and object relations theory may well be past (Shor and Sanville, 1985), and we may be reminded that "in the individual's mental life someone else is unvariably involved, as a model, as an object, as a helper, as an opponent . . . " (Freud, 1921, SE XVII, p. 69). Perhaps certain new trends can begin to bridge the gap between theory and practice. A current focus on "intersubjectivities" (Stolorow and Lachman, 1984, 1985) and on counter-transferential (Loewald, 1978) and iatrogenic complications (Gill, 1982, 1988; Stone, 1981) brings us all closer to a constructive concern with the inner experience of the psychotherapist and patient.

Transcending contentiousness among the schools of theory, I see a greater tolerance for a variety of subjective explorations of private qualities and quantities of experiencing. It is the "official" attitude towards an image of traditional clinical method and practice which is delaying deeper progress. Even a pioneer observer and theoretician like Blatt (1987) declares that "we are not suggesting any alteration of classic analytic technique" (p. 289).

These essays approach the subjective processes in both patient and therapist in critical detail, questioning principles implicit and hidden in traditional techniques and methods. Working suggestions for revising our ways in practice are considered and illustrated in vignettes. The influence of teachers and other colleagues will be evident. We each select and construct our own "Freud"; so also for all of the sources and authorities we adopt, both those identified and those not admitted to recognition.

There can be no doubt that Freud frequently patronized the image of a scientific psychology while he recurrently recognized non-predictable processes emerging in his therapy data. He ventured into metapsychological formulations but also reported unanticipated clinical events. We cannot assign Freud to either the scientific or the humanistic position; he oscillated, hoping to close the gaps between bio-neural phenomena and private psychological experiencing.

While neuro-science and genetics work to identify the parallel processes and variables in brain-mind functioning, the clinical psychotherapist presumes to practice with the subjective qualities and quantities of mental experience presented by willing patients. Even with involuntary clients, the psychological data can emerge to overrun the frames of our ever-changing theories as though the human spirit resists any set boundaries, even beyond conventional play. Much as we may diagnose, predict, and work for cohesion and order, and achieve synthesis, reconstructions and narratives, the experienced patient moves on to fresh explorations and reaches for novelty, "perfection" and the unknown. Our current concepts of "play" and "meaning," our theories about wishes, fears, drives and motives, are soon to be undone and the person ventures into open-ended evolution. Freud approaches this problem in his very last article (1940, SE XXIII, pp. 271–278) on "Splitting of the Ego." One may wonder when and how neural research will be ready to consider such clinical phenomena as creative fantasy experiencing and anticipating, so vital in my approach. REM dream studies may seem promising but are clinically questionable. (See Chapter VIII).

Meanwhile, ongoing psychotherapy develops psychological ways to meet with the potentially infinite complaining and searching inherent in the human condition; we also see evidences of a capacity to repair and reverse some "basic faults" (Balint, 1968) as some neurologists begin to discover that neural structures and damage may sometimes be reversible (M. Diamond, 1988 and A. Scheibel, 1989). My emphasis is on clinical processes rather than on metapsychology or neurology. Yet theories from humanistic data can be tentative hypotheses which the patient may find to be useful cues for self exploring and self reflecting when he invites our interpretations.

The central idea which I propose is the hypothesis of primary and persistent qualities of a dialogue in development and in psychotherapy. The specialness of this dialogue derives from the explicit sense of private complaint and desire in the person who initiates the relationship and from his explicit hope to modify or repair the quality of private experiencing in a significant aspect of life. The patient is basically "in charge" but engages the psychotherapist to offer his best hypotheses for consideration. This model is an ideal; widespread compromises and concessions limit the potential depth and comprehensiveness of the psychotherapeutic process, in my view, but the renewal of "in charge" experiences in the patient through negotiation may be preliminary and prerequisite. Such "new beginnings" (Balint) correspond to "rerailing the dialogue" (Spitz) in child-parent interplay. The criteria are located in a fuller consciousness of hidden complaints and desires. The most profound psychotherapy evokes awarenesses of a primary model of "perfect" fulfillment; such recognitions renew the impetus and guide the fresh efforts for reforming self and relationships.

My chief concern here is with the complexities of clinical practice aiming for that ideal dialogue within psychotherapy. The core experience of complaint provokes a changing variety of thrusts and measures called 'defenses'. The expression of dissatisfaction challenges our social resources which shape the responses to the clamor. We can see cultural progress as the expansion of sensitive tolerance and empathy for the emerging (Stern, 1985, et. al) if ambiguous messages of the infant and other later, yet still primary states of utterance and communication, both creative and pathological. What varies is our reading of these reports and intelligences and our felt readiness to recognize, imagine and foster a person's reaching for and exploring our resources and its own.

What assumptions and anticipations do we offer to guide the care we give in response? The clinician needs cues and hypotheses from theories in psychotherapy and from direct observations, though both activities lack the degree of reliable control and prediction idealized in the physical sciences. We draw upon our own humanistic framework. Are there basic and inevitable complaints in the human condition? How do such complaints work to shape the individual and his/her relationships and to give meanings to the phases of living and of dying? Erik Erikson's work on the dialectic of developmental stages has been most helpful to me in these directions.

The traditional scientific and technological criteria of prediction and control will gain little support here. One can view science as a product of our efforts to gain a degree of safe space, not as an ultimate aim or model for experiencing the human condition. Such safety may allow psychotherapy to be a process for self liberation, not a set of mechanistic "techniques" or benign manipulations. The first psychoanalytic hint of this perspective was evident in Freud's report of his very first clinical case study in psychotherapy, Emmy von N. (1895, *Studies in Hysteria*):

31

I requested her to remember by tomorrow. She then said in a definitely grumbling tone that I was not to keep on asking her where this and that came from but to let her tell me what she had to say. I fell in with this, and she went on without preface. . . . After I had spoken some calming words about what she had told me, she said she felt better. . . . [The next day] She was in a good mood. . . . She asked me my opinion about all sorts of things that seemed to her important . . . [but] she became agitated when I prepared to do massage. (S.E. II, p. 63).

He sums up later (p. 92) that the cue to fluctuations of symptoms is in the "self feeling" of the patient.

Freud's respect here signifies a modesty about the role of scientific prediction of psychodynamics. He is contending with the private, subjective data in psychotherapy. This complication permeates the professional task. Freud grapples with the difficulty recurrently:

It is true that we are unable to measure this amount of libido which seems to us indispensable for a pathogenic effect; we can only postulate it after the resulting illness has started (SE XII, p. 236).

From a knowledge of the premises we could not have foretold the nature of the result . . . what we know about them is only their quality, and not their relative strength . . . to predict it . . . is impossible (SE XVIII, pp. 167–168).

Clearly, it [the essence and meaning of a danger situation] consists in the subject's estimation of his own strength compared to the magnitude of the danger and in his admission of helplessness in the face of it. . . . In doing this he will be guided by the actual experiences he has had, whether he is wrong in his estimation or not is immaterial for the outcome (SE XX, p. 166).

Here it is not easy to predict a natural end to the process . . . the business of analysis is to secure the best possible conditions for the functioning of the ego; when this has been done, analysis has accomplished its task (SE XXIII, p. 250).

We are left with a heritage which challenges us to develop clinical methods and a psychotherapeutic atmosphere which liberate the patient to recover his own hidden forces and to reconstruct his capacities and ways of understanding and managing them, at his own pace of repair. That model will not satisfy the criteria of the traditional scientist. Yet Freud's humanistic attitudes, in depth, are my starting points, my prime assumptions and anticipations in experiencing psychotherapy, as patient and as therapist.

Some colleagues have disagreed with such optimism; they see a more primary place for evil, destructiveness and tragedy in the human experience. They favor a tragic view of life, a darker clamour about the human condition and its prospects. They warn me: "Your view may be kind, but it is naive and even dangerous. You neglect some ineffibly deeper forces which require our maintaining a careful professional responsibility. *We* should remain in charge, not the patient." Karl Menninger (1957) essentiallly took this position in spite of his thesis of a contract between patient and therapist; he calls this "a paradox" not yet resolvable. M. Eigen updates the cautionary attitude, but he also leaves the therapeutic challenge tautly open: "We cannot be too careful in our explorations of the capacities which constitute us" (1989, p. 627). I choose to take care that *the patient* make freer measures of his private experience rather than to take over that task for him. The pessimistic authoritarian view may seem justified by historical and sociological data about social and political disasters as well as by reports of clinical data on relentless suffering from *so far* unanswerable complaints and still active distrusts hidden in persisting fantasies, dreams and nightmares.

Those tragic approaches can enhance the drama on the couch and aim to arm the psyche for every encounter within and outside the Self; little room is left for free play in life. The rationale for these grim concerns may foster a professional resignation which restricts the patient's search for more perfect safe space. Balint has enriched and sharpened the clinical challenge to such tragic stasis in his writings on *The Basic Fault*

33

(1968); he offers cues to a pathway through severe malignancies to benign regressions and to free "new beginnings." (1932).

I cannot deny or disprove the darker forces that may be discovered or uncovered in clinical practice, but I do question their original and ultimate powers. I cannot deny others' rights to defy hopes and to distrust given promises of peace and fulfillment. The reassurances of pollyannish messages are usually belittling to the spirit and the adventure of living with the contingencies and chaos which occur unpredictably. The therapeutic issue is the response to malignant regressions and the facilitating of a benign renewal of fresh efforts. Unobstructive empathy may clear the ameliorative path.

My position is between that of the benign, authoritarian protector and of the sympathizing, consoling leveler so that the patient makes his way as he seeks to regulate his/her own experiencing to meet and fulfill self measured preferences and potentialities. I cannot know in advance the limitations or possibilities of each client. There is work and responsibility enough to estimate and be responsible for my own dynamics and dimensions; my efforts here may protect the patient from untoward intrusions and impositions and may best provide a space, a place for his best efforts in her own behalf. If the client is convinced that my intents are not invasive, then, when I fail, I more likely will be forgiven and we each renew our efforts, side by side and together. In this dialogue approach, more unspeakable hidden forces may be converted and given clearer voice.

When the patient senses me lagging in the responsible work, he may allow my catching-up with his patience. I cannot promise or predict an ongoing usefulness for the dialogue. He may put me aside, appropriate to his measures of himself or of my relevance. The "customer" is always right (A. Lazare, 1975.); but he may be flexible and also change his mind. Our working together is an open process, a form of constructive illusion, perhaps potential and desired for all social relating and private experiencing. One may "play" with tragic themes rather than submit and commiserate.

What about the self-destructiveness of suicidal patients who aim for eternal silence, without dialogue? They cannot be prevented from a final act unless they signal a call for help within earshot as part of any felt threat of suicide. We can hear the threat as a call for connecting at greater depths, for a more elemental empathy, a more primary dialogue. After negotiating a safe, respectful working alliance, I try to evoke fuller expression of the dark complaints, bitter protests and anxious hopes; these opened feelings and images may evoke cues to more primary desires in living, not death. We cannot inject the wish to live where there is no trace, no arc of energy moving in search of actual desire. To presume we can create the wish to live is more burden that I would assume. To hope we may fan that element of positive spark is the impetus for offering a delicate dialogue with careful empathy, persistently and patiently. Szasz (1986) offers a harsher edition of this view.

I make the assumption that the evil is secondary, a product of previous failures in primary love (Balint) and thus ultimately less paralyzing or irreversible. Some drama may seem lost, but only that pressured or imposed on the scene; these are iatrogenic tragedies. The tragic view of humanity may be explored in freer, less paralyzing, symbolic forms, as tests and warnings; it is a potentially malignant image which need not finally overwhelm the benign illusion of the ongoing, hopeful primary dialogue with those who survive and continue experiencing patienthood in living. Without the dialectics of exchange, there is no sense of future. One cannot remain only what is present. Freud early joined Darwin in this view of open-ended evolution (Shor, 1963).

The prime emphasis in these essays is clearly located in issues of the workings of negotiation, respect and empathy, prior to interpretations, which should be invited, not imposed from without. These are all aspects of the ethics of the relationships between patient and therapist. But good manners of treatment are not enough; there is also the task of locating and defining the functioning places for the theories which constitute the bulk of psychoanalytic literature and training, even if the traditional clinical and case seminars in the education of the psychoanalyst may imply principles of professional relationship which have remained closely modelled on an image of orthodox classical "techniques," a stereotype which Freud neither practiced nor recommended. Our theories of pathological development and of unconscious mechanisms of "resistance," defense and adaptation are the sources of our tentative hypotheses about primary complaints and desires gone off track. But a sense of ethical correctness does work to fortify larger ambitions, the renewal of efforts to repair.

Let me anticipate another challenge or question about the adequacy of an emphasis on the ethics of the relationship for a significant therapeutic experience. For all the notes of pleasant, decent, respectful interaction that may follow from the approach put forth, one is asked: But how does basic change occur to justify the patient's efforts to resolve his complaints and to reach new qualities or potentialities in living? This is the question reached by A. Goldberg (1987) in his close consideration of "Psychoanalysis and Negotiation"; he ends with an essentially cognitive note: " . . . the job of getting another person to change involves an empathic exchange wherein each participant becomes aware of the other's position." However, Self psychology may lack the valuing of fusion feelings which I emphasize as a necessary stage. I sense a similar shyness in most contributors to a high level workshop on *How Does Treatment Help?* (Rothstein, 1988)

When empathy helps the patient feel that it is safe and "good enough" to proceed more deeply, he may come to explore further his complaints and desires. When he reaches a puzzle, a block, a stalemate to his search, he will feel freer to invite the therapist's suggestions. As he considers the gently given hypotheses, he may offer objections and criticisms. The sensitive professional will attend and modify his tentative interpretation to relate the signs of criticism to a larger hypothesis. If such exchanges advance the patient's consenting to try out and perhaps incorporate the ideas suggested, and the refining of his self-perspective or narrative, such negotiations increase the bond between the two. These confirmations of developing dialogue yield moments of merging of understanding and notes of fusion are experienced. These are occasions of benign regression (Balint, 1959).

If the therapist continues to respect the patient's autonomy and pace of inviting interpretations, there is no insistent repetition of previous formulations and the patient will move more freely between feelings of connecting and of separating comfortably. The moments of merging and fusion are essential; they prepare him to try out the other's qualities and proceed to a selective identification and assimilating. These are the phases preceding the "transmuting internalization" (Kohut, 1977) which may signify the changes sought by the client. This condensed summary of the dynamics of satisfactory change through illusory merging is elaborated in detail in later sections; for me the new idea emerges from M. Balint's lifework.

I shall not hide behind long case studies, which compound and conceal the secret, selective variables in such data. Even Eissler (1965) concludes that "when an analyst reports his findings, they cannot be accepted on faith . . . " (p. 389). Freud's detailed clinical reports have sometimes illustrated his sense of uncovering a new hypothesis about pathological development or his fresh recognition of an obstacle, a "resistance" to his emerging method of treatment. He avoided attempts to demonstrate any continuous, complete psychotherapy. All case reports are seriously reflective of the selective workings of memory and reconstruction; also, most of us would agree with the view that any recording is a significant intrusion into subtle private exchanges. Rather have I looked for some principles of the ethics of Freud's approach to the patient, and for hints of some general hypotheses about primary motivational dynamics in a setting in which one person asks another for help about his own private, subjective experiencing.

It is the inter-play between a set of ethical abstractions and an evolving model of patient-directed psychodynamic processes in psychotherapy which comprehend my sources, my aims and my objects in this frankly personal and subjective work. The overlapping strands in this professional narrative may burden its style in some chapters; one may credit or blame the very specialized way of life, a psychoanalytical life that has been mine since 1935, with some significant costs, of course. But the essential open-ended "dialogue continues" (Berger, 1987, p. 273 summing up his significant survey of *Clinical Empathy*).

IV

Sources of the Clinical Dialogue

The meaning of words like "dialogue" is transformed in time, as are the processes of dialogue themselves. Old language gets overloaded, used up and contaminated, and previous functions are recast into fresh phases of purpose, exchange and satisfaction. We feel a need to invent new terms or to make unaccustomed redefinitions. With the ever variable pace and direction of change, the effort for linguistic precision yields confusion and ambiguity; ongoing communication requires cycles of accommodation and assimilation (Piaget). We have begun to appreciate the mutual learning necessary in the patient-therapist interaction, and psychoanalytic theories increasingly attend to hidden slants and slides undercurrent in the professional meetings as we each search for further significances.

We need to be open to unexpected reaches of experience. If we allow for the unpredictable, we must hold our words, our assumptions, anticipations and offerings, lightly, flexibly, in the potential clinical interplay, verbal and non-verbal, intended and unconscious. How do we prepare ourselves and our clients for the possibilities of both bottomless pits and infinite ascensions?

The traditional analytic approach began with the classical model for absolutely free associations. This rule suggest an unearned freedom which is like the promise of primary love (Balint). But I see such instruction as problematic now that we increasingly can recognize how it presumes the patient's readiness, and probably ours as well. Also, to *instruct* a voluntary client ignores the advantages of making prior negotiations and private preparations. Rules or suggestions about procedures invade the self directed capacities for spontaneous dialogue. There is not yet the relationship, the trust, the attunement; resistance would be an appropriate reaction. Our traditional roles as experienced authorities and as benign resources reinforce that instructional model, unfortunately.

A century later there may be evolving a comprehensively broader model derived from cues suggested by experienced patients and supported by exciting new data from current observations of early infants. I believe that a special form of dialogue may now be delineated for psychodynamic psychotherapy which can recognize certain current hypotheses about the new patient and the newborn. It is fitting that we have moved from the term "Ego," to the label "Self" and are beginning to assert the word "person" in our professional literature with greater frequency.

First Appearances of a Person—A Primary Model of Exchange

A cultural historian may well restate much of human history by making a detailed review and analysis of the changing assumptions about the psychological state and potentialities of the newborn infant. A series of permeating differences are surely to be found between male and female points of view related to their variable roles and functioning.

In broad strokes the man has been fighting and grappling to create more safe space for gathering and cultivating supplies, for self expression and for exchange; he also has been hunting to provide some specially vital resources, while the woman has been nurturing the family, teaching expressiveness and refining exchange (Shor, 1970). Undercurrents of projective identification have served to yield and, by its possessiveness, to preserve for both males and females some glimpses of the sharing, merging and fusion which renew the hope for the primary illusion fulfillment at the core of enriched adult loving mutuality (Shor and Sanville, 1978). Meanwhile, he and she would probably formulate different images of the infant's psyche as each adult projects his or her own complaints and desires.

We are learning about the subtle ways by which the woman has been influencing and supporting the man's more evidently active and assertive functioning. The old patterns for joint but specialized partnership are challenged by the current movements towards more comprehensive opportunities for actual equalities. Already we see some signs that the feminist and the chauvinist are both modifying their views about human potentialities, but we also admit we have far to go.

We have not even solved the problem of finding a comfortable, non-sexist term for referring to the gender of the patient or the therapist in our professional discussions (Frank and Treichler, 1989). Facing this dilemma here, I am conceding a faulty practice as I generally choose to use the generic "he," "his," and "him" with a self-conscious sense of compromise.

For the larger question of differential cultural attitudes to the neonate's psyche, a hugh project for psychohistorical research, I do feel a strong conviction that a promising new model is beginning to be recognized from infant observations. These essays are my attempt to exercise that model in the clinical data of the patient and the therapist experiencing psychotherapy. To highlight this part of the project, I begin with a brief contrast between the emerging viewpoint and its predecessors.

I am not equipped to discuss the various conceptions about the absolutely inherent self or soul, which characterize the many religious faiths and philosophical formulations. A passing allusion to John Locke's doctrine of the "tabula rasa," the blank sheet image of the baby's mind, permits some appreciation of the attempt, in Western civilization, to mediate and refine the conflict between environmentalistic and innate constitutionalistic emphases. This, now traditional, polarization of nature versus nurture is gaining new data and methods of investigation as we identify the open dynamics in the genetic crucible and the ongoing interactive processes within the actual bio-psychosocial milieu.

William James came forth at the beginning era of scientific study in psychology with his impressionistic idea of a "blooming-buzzing confusion"; his deconstructive image does re-open the field for a fresh attention to provide experiential qualities beginning with a global cross dimensional aura (Blatt, 1987). In fact, James' *Varieties of Religious Experience* (1902) is rich with intuitive forerunners of psychodynamics which are now ready to be rediscovered and refined in the contexts of recent infant observation and psychoanalytic therapy, and James' insights are well worthy of mining for further hypotheses. Other views compete. I am less familiar with the clinical usefulness of the Behaviorists' concept of the black box of consciousness; and there are several related approaches in cognitive, information and systems theories which may add relevant parameters surrounding the central sense of self.

Nearly a century of psychoanalytic speculations in this realm has yielded an array of viewpoints, which may represent selective emphases at certain stages of early development and theory construction rather than a comprehensive conception of the original, innate psyche: Freud's changing views about instinctual or undifferentiated *ID*, primary narcissism, oceanic feelings, Abraham's pre-ambivalent passive oral phase, Ferenczi's passive object-love, Rank's idealization of the fetal state, Groddeck's inherent organic models.

I may become more interpretive as I list more current schools of thought which tend to be simplistically summarized in slogans, especially by opponents: M. Klein's greedy brat and paranoid schizoid phases dominated by part-object impulses and images, Mahler's autistic and symbiotic beginning states, Hartmann's neutral and autonomous ego energies and functions, Fairbairn's emphasis on clinging relatedness. Even Winnicott, among the British Independents, sometimes seems to give priority to an object relations image in his heralding of the mother-child unit, though his clinical reports have substantial regard for the private, subjective autonomous experiencing of one's self and of the other within a potential dialogue. Erikson (1964) postulates a first stage of the psyche as permeated with hope and trust. Kohut sees the self as "born strong, not weak . . . born into the psychological matrix of responsive self objects . . . " (1981, p. 157).

Perhaps we can see each of these views as sometimes manifest in neonate behavior, and all as partly correct cues to the private experience in our patients, whether introduced by the client or imposed by the therapist. Gill (1982, 1988) has been alerting us to method induced, iatrogenic symptoms and transferences, as have others such as Stone (1981) and Loewald (1978). My emphasis on the dialogue is intended to identify and develop a framework and a further tool for our professional efforts. If we can substantiate a primary capacity for exchange and for self repair, our work may be guided to be more effective, and perhaps less "impossible" (Freud, 1937).

Since Spitz's original work on infant smiling as a social exchange, many impressive films have been recording elements of dialogue in the first months of life, especially from the research groups at the University of Colorado, where he spent his last decade of work. Wolff (1959) had identified the easy alert states of the newborn. More recent studies by Trevarthan (1984), Stern (1985) and Blatt (1987) have described details of "resonance" and of "attunement" as mutually responsive communicating at very early ages. Many other approaches from this direction are presented in the 1982 volume by E. Tronick (Edit) on *Social Interchange in Infancy.*

Most impressive to me was the film, *The Amazing Newborn,* produced by M. Hack in 1975. It demonstrates flexible eye and hand contact with the mother within two hours after birth: "The sensory capabilities for interaction and exchange are clearly manifest." We see the immediate ability to oscillate, at a self-directed pace, between turning or moving towards the other and turning away. Implicit in such behaviors is some measuring of inner drives or intents to connect and also to disconnect; these private decisions are apparently reversible as the contact is sought, and then averted. The parents in the film are to be seen as available, gently friendly, responsive and non-intrusive; they are respecting the self-determinations and autonomy of the infants. There are signs of a negotiating between two persons.

From such interplay we may derive cues to a model of flexible seeking and retreat, for psychotherapy, from the first contacts. One remembers Freud's late proposal that therapy rests on the recovery of the "lost element of historical truth" (1937), since "object-finding is really a refinding" (1905). It would follow that our prime professional task is to facilitate the rediscovery of that primary position as a confident negotiator ready to develop a dialogue.

Developing Encounters with Contingencies and Illusions

As the caretakers, and the therapist, offer appropriate conditions for felt comfort and confidence, the emerging person reaches and stretches to know the unfamiliar world at hand. Phyllis Greenacre has described such processes of *Emotional Growth* (1959) when the caretaker facilitates the infant's learning and absorbing new levels of maturing. Winnicott (1971), Kestenberg (1978) and Stern (1985) have advanced and detailed these processes, with crucial significances for the theory of infant development.

Michael Balint has offered a broader set of clinical hypotheses from such ongoing developments, rooted and guided by a fuller model of exchanging in adult psychotherapy. Successful negotiations are experienced with joy: "This supreme happiness is to a very large extent an illusion, based on a regression to an infantile stage of reality testing" (1947, in *Primary Love and Psychoanalytic Technique*, 1952). He formulates the larger assumption more dynamically in 1959:

> Primary love is a relationship in which only one partner may have demands and claims; the other partner (or partners, i.e. the whole world) must have no interests, no wishes, no demands, of his or her own. There is and must be, a complete harmony, i.e., a complete identity of wishes and satisfactions (p. 22).

This 'illusion' (from *in ludere,* in play) is supported by the caretaker, also the therapist, to the limits of her capacities and resources for fitting attunement and empathy; such abilities depend upon processes in the adult which derive from a comfortable, flexible, cohesive self available to play with primary illusion (Shor and Sanville, 1978). If well met, the primary person can be seen to be experiencing three basically different qualities of self reference: ME, MYSELF and I.

Three Experiential Levels of Personhood: Me, Myself and I

In 1905 Freud offered his classical hypothesis about the three phases of the human drive (*treib*): source, aim, and object. He recognized a preliminary biological input as the impetus to the unfolding of "instinct," but wanting to explore fully the potentialities of his new psychological method, he determined to proceed "in conflict with the official science" (1913) of his day. Since then psychoanalysis has been increasingly developing concepts which are based in certain "universals" of the human experience prior to inevitable cultural differentiations, but seeing these commonalities as so shaped and formed by the cultural that the person becomes a bio-psycho-social being. However, the person is not only molded by the culture, but is engaged in actively modifying the surround. Freud's schema has ongoing merit as a way of viewing both the persons who seek psychoanalytic help and the socio-cultural milieu in which they live, work, and relate to other.

Source, for Freud, alluded to the sense of supply of psychic energy (soon to be called libido), energy which was capable of a quantitative charge of vitality in the experiencing of self. *Aim* referred to the pathways of discharge of that energy along variable lines of physiological functioning available to the organism. *Object* encompassed all the representations of external stimuli in relation to which the energy discharge was experienced. In the course of development the infant must first feel secure in basic supplies before it can begin to function, and must experience a certain independence in functioning before being able to interrelate with others seen as separate from the self. Certain qualities are first manifested in these developmental stages, but later will be experienced as recurrent and often overlapping states. It is likely that every fresh biological impetus of a maturational nature may go through all of these psychological phases: first reaching for a quality of vitality (*source* as supply), finding a pathway to move via body ego with skill and pleasure (*aim* as functioning), and then seeking social contexts for ways in which these accretions may be included in relationships with others (*object* as exchange). It becomes a spiral dialectic of accommodations and assimilations (Piaget).

Me (the "oral" attitude)

Following Balint, Shor and Sanville (1978) have proposed that human life begins in a sort of "primary illusion," a dreamlike state in which there is but a virtual sense of self, gently oscillating with a virtual sense of other, not yet with any felt conflict between the two. Whatever "representation" may go on is at first largely in bodily terms; and the *me* is ideally experienced as the contented receiver of good supplies which dissolve all felt tensions or "needs." There is simply a sense of effortless abundance without conditions or limits, and a resultant easy bliss. This initial contented state, it is assumed, must make its imprint on the neural apparatus in such a way as to become a model toward which all subsequent reparative impulses aim. Just as the body comes to know its own wholeness and when ill or injured strives to regain that intactness, so the psyche "knows" this blissful condition and when there is a fall from paradise, as there must inevitably be, will attempt to reconstitute both self and its surround to make possible new and increasingly complex versions of the *primary illusion.*

That cycle is inherent in the beginning dialogues between baby and mother. In the "oral" phase the infant is not simply passive, but actively exchanges with the caretaker. Life begins, as Spitz (1963) affirms, with the dialogue. Within this process, moments of successful meeting and fusion with the other lead to selective identifications which enrich the *self* of the infant and encourage an ever-expanding sense of functioning, and to increase the capacity for exchange. The cycle is not just repetitious but the Me, Myself and I becomes a dialectical spiral because of these fulfillments in merging; the entire sequence of phases may constitute the stages of complete love. Freud (1905) perhaps laid the ground for this spiral of psychic growth when he wrote "There are thus good reasons why a child sucking at his mother's breast has become the prototype of every relation of love. The finding of an object is in fact a refinding of it" (p. 45).

The "pathology" which may first arise in this first stage of life, ME, and which may recur later, is identified in the clinical situation when the patient expresses in the transference paranoid and schizoid terrors about basic scarcities. These anxieties give rise to fantasies of inner-outer attack, and abandonment, of fragmentation and dissolution of the self, such as are manifest in schizophrenia or in primary (anaclitic) depressions. The *deprived* person may experience and sometimes vent rages against both self and therapist when not feeling supplied for basic needs. Kohut (1972) describes violent eruptions of isolated destructiveness after injury to a fragmenting or almost destroyed self. The dictionary (American Heritage) defines rage as violent anger; akin to a *fit;* or as furious intensity "as of a storm or disease." The word thus connotes something of an involuntary global response, not yet refined or directed, a sort of all-or-none phenomenon. It is perhaps the extreme negative side of what Spitz (1965) calls the coenesthetic, in which "sensing is extensive, primarily visceral, centered in the autonomic nervous system, and manifests itself in the form of emotions" (p. 44). The emotions are not yet felt to be either controllable or directable, but rather as having the potential for terrible, overwhelming destructiveness. Thus one patient used to speak of the rage, not as "owned" by her, but as a "dark cloud descending," and when shrouded in its fog she lost all ability to perceive self or other, or to think. She would say, "I feel nothing—and I don't know who you are"; thus both self and other were obliterated by the storm.

It follows that the therapeutic approach is always to include in any interpretive comment a reference to the reparative thrust which can be identified in the symptom; this works to make conscious the *basic wish*, which is not originally a destructive one. When the person is manifesting felt *deprivation* he or she is wanting the other to be a reliable and perfect source, one whose empathetic right timing in offering the needed qualities and quantities of supplies would permit absolute harmony to be taken for granted. When the other can be so experienced, the person moves to merge again, in the fantasy that fusion will facilitate incorporating into the sense of self qualities which will permit self-sustaining.

In certain faulty contexts the seeking after good mirroring results only in further deprivation, further blind rage. Thus the patient just mentioned would return from visits to her parents, reporting that when she tried to share an event of importance to her they had given no confirming response; she had felt "wiped out." Unable to idealize them she sought in a homosexual alliance the "perfect" other, in spite of frequent dissonance, and attempted by self-distorting submission to modify and repair the hoped-for *source*. To "read" her symptom in this way, rather than as, for example, a masochistic acting-out, is to enable her to know more clearly what she seeks and hence to make a better measure of the *ways* she might select to fulfill her wish.

Myself ("anal" and "phallic-hysteric" qualities)

In the course of development, when the infant has felt "at one with" a good enough caretaker, it is ready for experimentation with separate functioning, and begins to do for self what was once done for it by the mother. The latter now becomes the "environmental mother" (Winnicott, 1963) and under ideal conditions is *there*, available for protection, approval, encouragement, validation of self expression. The child moves toward increasingly independent exercise of unfolding capacities and functions, with increasing initiative and pleasure in growing skills.

48

"Pathology" may result under a number of conditions: 1) if the caretaker is overanxious, unwilling to let the child out of sight, 2) is intrusive, intervening and directing instead of allowing and encouraging the child to be self-determining, 3) is neglectful, not providing safety and instruction, or 4) is given to adversely criticizing and discouraging the child's autonomous efforts. Under all these conditions the child may experience a sense of suppression. Space is not safe; it may even be dangerous. The child feels self doubt and sometimes shame at inability to measure and manage in the "world out there." Particularly when suppression is superimposed on a person already suffering from a sense of inadequate supplies, the reaction can still be a "narcissistic" rage, an agitated depression, or even a sense of paranoid-schizoid oppression. Otherwise the furies tend to be somewhat tamed by now, shaped; angers take the form of expression of extreme displeasure, indignation, exasperation with the thwarting one.

Many patients complain about not being allowed to function in a way that is satisfactory. One young woman, employed in a department store, seeks treatment because of chronic depression which she connects with an inability to choose a career. She hates her present work, in spite of having been awarded regular promotions. Her hours are long, the tasks arduous and dull, and, to her, meaningless and insignificant. She is so exhausted at the end of each day that she cannot even indulge in private activities she might enjoy. Her life, she feels, is becoming like that of her father, who was so busy earning a good living for his family that he had no time for the family. On a practical level she could move away from this occupation to another, for her parents would pay for additional schooling, finance her in her own business, help in any of these facilitating ways. Her problem is that she keeps herself in this unpleasurable situation, fearful of any new decision lest it foreclose on alternative possibilities.

From time to time she becomes enraged with her therapist for not telling her what to do. And the therapist gently reminds her that she has been directed by parents—by father toward business, by mother toward the arts; yet here she is requesting that another person steer her. The reparative wish is to be able to express and develop her own capacities and functions, to find an arena which will permit some experimentation, so that she can risk both failure and success. I "read" her indecision as designed to prevent the solution chosen by father—to sacrifice togetherness for the sake of personal achievement, and that of mother—to devote self to others to the extent that is precluded individual development. The conflict is one which is present in one form or another in many of today's patients of both sexes, as they strive to transcend traditional sex roles.

I ("genital" qualities)

When the developing individual has been able to internalize the experiences with a good source, and with an interpersonal milieu that has encouraged independent functioning, he/she can then claim a strong sense of agenthood. This leads to the wish to share from the sense of abundances, and to seek reciprocal validations with others, that give and take which can promote fantasied mergings on new levels.

Most often the "pathologies" on this level have to do with the tendency of many people to leap to connections with others before they have sufficiently consolidated the confidence in self, both as source and as container. Thus they come to experience themselves as rejected, belittled. They then react with disappointment, become depressed under some circumstances, as when they feel critically devaluated as to the adequacy of supplies or of their ability to skillfully function; they may regress to earlier feelings of being a damaged self, be unable to do things well. But when the disappointment is not too severe they may be moved to renewed efforts to improve supplies and skills and to reach for another partner.

So far I have focused, and in a very condensed manner, on the "failures" that, in therapy, become the complaints which patients present to us, as they seek to repair their felt deprivations, suppressions, and frustrations which are the burdens of the Me, Myself, and I. In normal and pathological mourning and also in the variety of depressive states, the hidden problems may also be found to be these three levels of "loss" being experienced.

What would represent "success"? What is the model of the potential ideal human condition? We have already suggested that when persons feel that they are adequately supplied (first by an outer and then by an internalized *source*), they then seek the pleasure of exercising developing functions and skills (aim), and when they have attained a sense of mastery, they then want to exchange, to share resources and to participate with a valued other or others (object). When exchange is rewarding they experience mutuality, moments of fantasized merging which are new versions of the primary love of infancy. They imaginatively take into themselves the valued qualities of the other and experience an enhanced sense of self out of this identification. In the swing of this dialectic they then wish to try out the new qualities in some area of autonomous functioning, and they are ready to risk further explorations by themselves "out there" in the world. There will be inevitable times of feeling depleted of supplies, times of discovering inadequacies to the challenges undertaken. These experiences will motivate fresh reachings for relationships which can replenish and for situations in which they can develop and hone the needed skills (such as education or training, where it can be safe to return to the status of learner).

One may see life as proceeding along the pattern of a dialectical spiral or double helix. Phases of togetherness will alternate with phases of autonomy, and when movement is not blocked (from within or without), there will be times when the two lines of development, that of "narcissism" and that of "object relationships" will be very close—and adult editions of the primary illusion may be enjoyed. The central hypothesis is that there are, at the beginning, timeless moments of no conflict between togetherness and fusion, or separateness and autonomy. For the contented infant, there is no issue about this; there is simply a gentle oscillation between one state and the other, between attachment and withdrawal. Of course this original bliss cannot last. The intertwining illusions of "primary

51

narcissism" and of "primary love" (Freud and Balint) are both doomed to give way as the infant experiences inevitable deprivations, suppressions and frustrations at the hands of the caretakers. But the dis-illusions set in motion powerful reparative wishes, wishes to re-discover that primary bliss. The reparative efforts are at times directed toward the felt-to-be-damaged or inadequate self, at times toward the other person or persons, and again toward the social surround—aiming at the enlargement of the "zone of safety" (Balint, 1959).

We may remind ourselves that *illusion* means "in play" (*in ludere*) (Huizinga, 1944); its opposite being *delusion,* or "away from play." It is only in play or playfulness that a return to an infantile experience can be benign. Winnicott writes (1971): "Psychotherapy has to do with two people playing together. The corollary of this is that where playing is not possible, then the work done by the therapist is directed toward bringing the patient from a state of not being able to play into a state of being able to play" (p. 38). The therapist's initial task is to attend to the creation of a playground, a safe space in which the patient can reenact and restructure the three aspects of his "narcissism" and the "object relationships" which he/she needs and wants for the "me, myself, and I." To the degree we are successful, the patient becomes able to use the "transference as a playground," as Freud (1914) put it, casting us in the roles of the others who are wanted and/or feared, and discovering in this process the obstacles and the strengths in self, both that which hinders and that which might promote the success of the venture.

The adult who enters treatment rarely imagines that the experience with the therapist will be one of play. Years of accommodating to the social roles which have been assigned or selected, to viewing things and events logically and realistically, lead the person to expect that there will be a 'proper' patient-role too, and that problems must be tackled with diligence and earnestness. Play is seen as the domain of childhood, except of course for those activities which one may permit oneself as recreation, carried out in the brief time spans all too often felt to be stolen from more important pursuits. The therapist, like other "doctors," is expected to pre-scribe, not necessarily medicines, but "what to do" about that which is troublesome. Most adults, unlike children, are not ready at first to turn passive into active, to dose themselves, at their own pace, with memories of traumatic experiences, to use this situation to reclaim a lost agenthood. Others, espe-cially males, tend to be "fixated" on the instrumental role, and dread the expressiveness of patienthood, associating it with in-fancy and helplessness. But, although the play spirit may ap-pear to be maimed, it is never dead, and the therapist's efforts will be to liberate it: to enable the person to elude old roles and rules, to experience a sense of freedom in this situation and within self. The person who would re-order psyche, rela-tionships, or surround must risk breaking up old ways of being and doing; only then it is possible to create new arrangements which are more satisfying, even exciting.

Thus, in response to the complaints or "failures" which the patient presents, the therapist can now work to create a proper scene in which an exploratory attitude may emerge in the safe outer-inner space, a playground in which the patient will not be so earnest, but will relax and be able to communicate with both therapist and self. As the patient moves through various phases of the dialectic spiral between togetherness and auton-omy, there will be cues in the transference projections for the kind of *space* sought at different times. When the concern is with supplies for *Me*, the patient is likely to manifest a cling-ing, sometimes to the extent that it would seem that she wants to obliterate the space between self and the seen-to-be-powerful other. When the interpretive comment includes the wished-for inclusion of the imagined qualities of the other into the self, the person may move from the hope of achieving this in a magical way to actions which enable her to acquire in self the sought-for attributes.

Then the *space* will be experienced by both therapist and patient as expanding. If the patient is not to feel suppressed while developing the skills to "do it *myself*," then she must feel free to move away from the therapist. Sometimes this will be within the session—as by not talking, by letting herself partake of that "being alone in the presence of another" which Winnicott (1972) says is the necessary preface to the important capacity to be alone. Sometimes it will be by an occasional *interlude* (for some private play), a chosen interruption to test out and practice unfolding dimensions of the self. During these periods the sense of optimal *space* expands; the person wants to be free to move away at her own discretion, much as does the infant in the separation-individuation phase which Mahler et al (1975) described, but wants the therapist to stay available and accessible for the occasional refueling which may be desired.

When a sense of self as agent has been attained the "I" manifests a capacity for wide swings in what is felt to be optimal space at different times. For now the person is able to enjoy play with both illusions—that of fusion, when space between self and other is imaginatively dissolved and two becomes as one, and that of autonomy, when the whole world may be felt as a "friendly expanse" (Balint, 1959) in which to exercise seemingly limitless possibilities. It is likely at this time that the person decides to terminate therapy. But paradoxically, just because she has "progressed" she may also feel freer to "regress" should the vicissitudes of life reawaken old deprivations, suppressions and frustrations. She would be unlikely to experience a need to return to therapy as a severe narcissistic wound, for all along she has carried with her a memory and an image of a safe space in which adult play could yield growth and richer living, not only beyond any of the established diagnostic categories of pathology, but even beyond what she had so far believed or known to be possible.

A Dialectic Spiral of Phases of Personhood

The following sequence is suggested as descriptive of the dialectical spiral of changes of personhood in psychosocial development; motivated by universal wishes to create fresh editions of a primary illusion, human beings aim at emending both versions of the self and versions of the culture which can provide a context for such re-construction.

1. Feeling adequately supplied (Source, for "Me")
2. Expressing functions and skills with pleasure (Aim, of "Myself")
3. Exchanging and sharing resources (Object,"I" seek)
4. Experiencing mutuality and mergings, with illusions of fusion (We—Us)
5. Incorporating identifications (for "Me")
6. Separating to autonomy ("Myself")
7. Further self expressions and risking explorations (Seeking new "I")
8. Inevitable depletions of supplies and capabilities (Knowing failures)
9. Reaching for new levels of object-relationship (Source, Aim, and Object)
10. Ongoing dialectical spiral or double helix, the dialogue process

In psychoanalysis, interpretations of the specific reparative wishes and obstructive fantasies of failure, hidden in each symptom and complaint as presented, can liberate moves to cease "derailing the dialogue" (Spitz, 1964) and can free next, new growth or discovery.

The avoidance of diagnostic labels can render the clinician more open both to the universalities and to the uniqueness in each person. An atmosphere of authoritarianism, however benign, can interfere with the sense of freedom which is the essence of playfulness. Still to be discovered are the subtle variations of complaint and hope in those patients traditionally called narcissistic personalities, schizophrenics, or depressives. Most important will be to learn the inner conditions of the analyst which are essential in applying this approach. As further advances are made, one may hope that psychoanalytic therapy can more effectively take its place at the frontiers of culture, facilitating an expanding and open-ended evolutionary process, rather than merely patching up deviations or accommodations to a culture and a society which are themselves experienced as needing repair and creative modification.

The psychotherapist meets with those who may be closer to protest or search for better inner or outer experiences, those who carry a burden of failed efforts in trying to do their own repairing. The residue of complaints, distrusts, compromises and hopes are the raw materials, in substantial part unconscious, for our work together. These patients are to be seen as possibly open for new efforts with us, aspiring to move from a passive suffering ME toward an active and curious MYSELF, and then a revitalized I, ready for the unpredictable vicissitudes of reaching for, meeting, exchanging with, merging and fusing, with easy, flexible partings and also renewals of the spiral—all with an equally valued other.

V

Patient Experiencing

However a patient initiates our contact, I have in mind a basic sequence of tasks for me as potential therapist: first, explicit negotiating on *all* practical aspects of the process; next, offering empathic comment on signs of ill ease in negotiating and then in presenting his complaints and wishes; and finally, when invited, making psychodynamic and transference interpretations. This sequence is renewed whenever the patient shows uneasy feelings. Here is how I try to develop our relationship into a working alliance.

A potential patient calls to make an appointment for a first consultation. I ask when he would like to come in, thus offering the note that his choice is the first consideration. He may demure and offer himself to my convenience. I ask his preferences. If none of them is possible for me, I suggest my alternatives. He is invited to choose amongst these. From such negotiations, the patient may also sense my flexible attitudes and my acceptance of responsibility for my private considerations. As he likely will manifest some forms of uneasiness around these seemingly practical parlays, I note this to him in a gentle inquiring tone in order to express my interest in whatever uncertainties he is experiencing. Thus, from the start, he can see me becoming specially alert to both his preferences and to any signs of his discomfort about asserting an easy self-directing manner. For simplicity, I here refer to the patient as of the masculine gender.

If he asks further questions, I respond directly if I think them reasonable and if I feel ready to reply simply, in a matter-of-fact manner; if not, I suggest we could discuss them when we meet. I limit that first inquiry by stating my readiness to explore the content of his questions when I can confirm with him the importance he feels about the specific details of any questions involving professional or private information about me he may ask. I express the hope, explicitly, that in meeting we may both exchange facts and considerations which will help us to decide whether and how we *may* work together. The permeating attitude is to view myself as a possible resource which he may choose to hire in his search for better answers for himself. I imply the essential assumption that I will view him in charge of all details and free to decide about accommodating to my explicit conditions, to negotiate compromises, or to leave at any time he chooses.

I remember how I was unable initially to offer these attitudes in the first years of practice. One control analyst had told me it was best to begin only when I had three or more potential patients so that I might distribute my anxious investment in a new professional identity. Another supervisor encouraged my waiting until I understood the principle that we make the fastest and deepest progress in analysis when we can feel as though we have infinite time available. It took years for such advices to be internalized and the pressures, inner and outer, to suspend these patient positions do recur to this day. And yet, if I make the effort to manifest modest and negotiating ways at the beginnings of the therapeutic relationship, there is an explicit point of reference which I think may be registered by the client at some primary level of his psyche and may nourish a basic hope for our working together toward *his* ultimate aims for *his own autonomy.* When I slip and act as though I want to be in charge, I can correct myself explicitly and the patient may well forgive me and work on with me; or he may not and leave.

The initial orientation with the patient will be reinforced as we meet and negotiate about the specific arrangements: fees, frequency of sessions, and the flexibilities I may agree to reconsider with him. I ask or await his expressed preferences on all details of arrangements. I aim to set a tone which suggests he may view our sessions as his time, his space, to explore whatever he may wish, and at his pace. While I will have indicated that I have my private considerations, my private schedule and subjective preferences, I feel no need to explain them, though if he asks, I may decide to share some reasons for setting my conditions. Within myself, I try to maintain a low-key manner, giving him the lead for making the atmosphere as safe for his self-reporting as he feels will be good enough.

My seemingly passive stance yet permits me to demonstrate that I can and intend to take care of my own autonomy and will try to be available to meet his explicit inquiries and his invitations to offer my best understandings as tentative hypotheses. A spirit of dialogue is offered, even as I sense his doubts and his demands for *my* leading the way.

Surely his neurotic processes will defy and even deny that friendly dialogue spirit I manifest in the negotiating. These distortions are usually seen as his transference neurosis but such repetitiveness may be viewed as a series of tests of my respecting his deeper reparative capacities. His difficulties with maintaining comfortable negotiating are the foci of my attempts to offer gently empathic inquiries.

If there are transference distortions, I do not interpret them at this early stage. I may register my recognition of his ignoring my offer and make occasion to restate the negotiation simply and wait quietly for his next move. If he continues to neglect the point of practical arrangement, I give my rationale for his fuller attention. A patient attitude here yields a further expression of his expectations and presumptions about how therapy would or should proceed. I correct his assumptions to state my preferred principles that we negotiate and that he is in charge of his side of the relationship.

There are constraints to his freedom, of course; and I am

responsible for my needs and interests, which I indicate only insofar as they limit him, which I say I regret I must impose for my sake. Such verbal exchanges are kept to a minimum so that he may, from the first contacts, experience glimpses, at least, of the freer, safer atmosphere I offer. Then his presentation of complaints might proceed with greater coherence and less self-belittling dependency.

I invite his thoughts and explanations about his presenting complaints. No life history data is requested, nor do I presume the right to ask about his past or his outside experiences. Beyond negotiating the arrangements, I am attending to the emotional tones in his inquiries, responses and accounts of his considerations, preferences and dissatisfactions; I am gathering hints about his feelings and attitudes in expressing himself to me, including cues form the non-verbal behaviors. I listen for implications about his sense of vital supplies, of freedom and pleasure in self expression and of felt opportunities to exchange and share with preferred others. My empathic comments are attempts to identify such qualities of discontent: deprivation, suppression and frustration. Yet I speak in a tentative spirit, more as inquiring then pronouncing.

I allow my interest in experiencing an attunement with these affects to be manifest in my own verbal and non verbal manners. When he turns to me, I offer gentle empathic comments to confirm that interest and to foster his continuing to deepen his self exploration. The emphasis on the patient's leading role does reduce the intrusion of my hypotheses in offering empathy. I wait to be asked, as Freud did with Emmy von N. (page 1).

No interpretations are given until the patient explicitly invites my understandings. This policy is controversial among close colleagues. My rationale is that the patient is learning to do self analysis and may surprise himself, and me, with his spontaneous discoveries in this special setting made safe by our consistent negotiating. A transference neurosis is less likely to develop. When he expresses confusion, or ambivalence or any puzzling about his inner distress, I make more delicate empathic comments as a model for self investigation. By waiting to offer my tentative interpretations until he makes explicit invitation, I show respect for his efforts and for his measures and self-pacing. He remains in charge of my participation. The analyst's investment and powers are not identical with those of the parent. The hired helper should and can afford to be more purely empathic and more patient.

When I do interpret, I try to maintain a low-key tentative style in voice and language, ready to be corrected, revised or met with a silence. No direct response is required. Reflection or registering of resentment or anxiety may be going on but in his time and his space. I listen silently for a further invitation to make a fresh interpretive comment.

When in doubt whether I am being invited to speak, I gather and refine my hypotheses, storing and reflecting on their possible interconnections, in silence, patiently, I hope (Reik, 1937). As he gathers his demands on me in the complex transference behaviors I am sensing, including anxious and angry silences, I do venture empathic remarks about the emotional tones only. I do not make psychodynamic interpretations about those feelings or about the content of his communication. My fix on the levels of empathy is aimed to stay at the surface of his experience in the hope he will appreciate my sensitivity to his complicated, unverbalized attitudes. Only when he does feel safe and free enough to put this level of private here-and-now experiencing into words and does invite my view of his pain and conflict, do I formulate a gentle interpretation with an inquiry for his refining, revising or confirming the interpretation.

Before discussing the kinds of interpretation I may offer and the recognition and "handling" of the possible transference aspects, I must mention a line of thinking on these subjects which began for me in 1953 (Coleman and Shor) and developed substantially in recent decades (Shor, 1972; Shor and Sanville, 1978). The principle is to see all transferences as unconscious tests of the prospects for positive repair experiences. A summary of this perspective is given in chapter XI; under "Self provocation and Reparation."

Of course, the basic functions of the therapist, negotiation, empathy and interpretation, may be called for in repeated cycles and dialectic spirals as the patient manifests transference regressions to test out previous gains in the relationship or to approach another problem element in his felt deficiencies, damages or conflicts. I let him take the lead at his pace. We negotiate at each level until the patient shows some easier self-directing in initiating the themes for consideration.

After a good piece of negotiation, a fragment of hidden feeling may be released and become more manifestly expressed. That bit can best be elaborated and associated to in the now more comfortable context so that the patient puts before us more elements of complaints and desires for our joint attention. I trust the patient's inherent reach for repair through better self reflection and his wish for my helpful ideas. His offerings of more feeling elements are cues for our careful, gradual empathic participation so that a closer working alliance can develop.

I believe that he is not ready to use psychogenetic interpretations until the friendly alliance is confirmed enough so that he begins to explore his own explanations and speculations about his problematic emotions and behaviors. His own reflective efforts may be very shy and circumspect until I renew my empathic stance and gradually introduce tentative hints about the possible reparative hopes and intents in his symptoms. The spontaneous search for meanings and purposes by the patient must be liberated, I believe, before he will invite the therapist, as ally, to give his hunches and enrich the joint reflective process. An indirect or disguised invitation should be met with some reflective empathy about this indirectness, not with a 'benign' leap to the presumed content in his uneasy reach. An uninvited interpretation risks a note of seduction or threat.

Thus, I never challenge or confront him, or "expose" his self deceptive mechanisms. Instead, I note to him some further feeling elements in the tones and style of his self expression and await his grappling with my empathic input. I am attending to his possible renewal of a self-exploring, self-directing attitude. With the loving implicit in the gentle empathy, I am fostering his sense of a warming, close bond between us and await his request for my participation in his background reflecting. Only then do I ready myself to offer, if invited, my best hypotheses from the realm of psychoanalytic theories which have permeated the professional training and literature that equipped my own general understandings. But my style in offering my thinking remains crucial. Though I try to be alert always to cues that he is looking to me for some response, I am often uncertain. I may offer my impression that he seems to be inviting or awaiting my comment on a specific question. Such explicit self consciousness adds options to his focus. I may add a note on the possible feeling tone in an invitation and in his presenting the issue to me. If he interrupts or ignores my remarks, I keep silent and listen for a next hint of invitation or confrontation, whether anxious, angry or pained.

So far, this schematic approach may seem labored and wasteful to the more active psychotherapist. It was T. Reik who suggested that we proceed as though we had all the time in the world. Even such advice is fraught with possible error and misjudgment on our part. Just as the patient is recurrently testing for our hidden agenda in his transference manifestations (Shor, 1972), we must remain alert to the qualities in the patient's response to our interventions (Freud, 1937) and be ready to pause, demur, renew or refine our empathic efforts to reestablish the bonds for a working alliance. Our readiness to retreat from interpretations to empathy and even to negotiating can signify a flexibility to improve the experiential relevance of a formulation; such openness can be a model for the patient who can sense that he is still in charge.

Against the background experience of my persisting, if gently, to negotiate as many of the practical arrangements as possible, instead of laying down any rules, I await this voluntary patient's reach for my empathic appreciation of and participation in his emotional dilemmas and stalemates. As he selects and paces his exposing of feelings, I show myself trying to resonate and attune first to the surface of his complaint and then to wait for his acceptance of such intimate gestures. If he responds with notes of resistance and fails to continue and deepen the reporting and describing, I retreat to note and hypothesize the presence of feelings of my having intruded too much, and I say so, softly, expecting and allowing him to regroup his defenses. I wait for his next gesture; if it is away from our alliance, I explicitly admit my fault. If he stays and then makes another move toward me, I now more carefully attend and empathize more softly until he resumes his forward self-expression.

As I detail here the efforts for empathic harmony, I am again moved to indicate my appreciation to L. Havens' contribution toward a fresh, comprehensive theory of empathy in his recent work on *Making Contact* (1986). During two years as Lecturer, alongside him, at the Harvard Department of Psychiatry, I have seen the therapeutic values of his sensitive refinements for many types and qualities of empathy with some original discriminations of "empathic language" and styles. His delicate approach to the realm of subjectivities promises great benefits for advancing through patient problems of "resistance" with fewer battling encounters or dogged stalemates. Berger (1987) has also made use of Havens' work.

Of course I avoid reassuring or advising the stuck, suffering patient. My applications of graded empathy aim to evoke his expression of a deepened awareness of complaints and desires; to these I gradually add tentative suggestions of the possible reparative goals implied or hinted. At first, my reflection of his immediate feeling tone may be distrusted and elicit retreats to a wary or hostile distance. A patient, even sad, silence on my part may be followed by a gentle inquiry whether I erred or intruded. I let him know he can limit and judge my manners toward him. My adapting mode is meant to elicit the hidden anxieties and hopes, the malignant and benign wishes and illusions, toward sharing and joint reflection in session or privately.

The previous chapter proposed the qualities of complaint (deprivation, suppression and frustration) and the dimensions of desire (enough supplies, self-expression and responsive exchange) for which I listen. These are the terms I introduce when the patient permits himself to elaborate his feelings of discomfort and of hope and also pauses for my comments. My

64

statements are surface interventions and we may proceed to refine and polish the feelings and meanings in accord. When he makes a passing comment which seems to me to be a transference distortion, I look up with a note of easy surprise but wait for the possible distortion to be repeated. My surprise may be slightly audible but no focus is made on the point until he repeats it and pauses for my notice. I raise the question whether his remark feels like an impression or a certainty. We negotiate on the question of exploring that idea. I am mindful of Gill's writings on the plausibility of the patient's view (1982, 1984, in Lichtenberg, p. 177, and 1988) on what we've called transferences. The open discussion encourages a mutual reflecting and evaluation. Sometimes I suggest my uncertainity of conclusion so that we might return to the issue at any later time he chooses.

When such mutual consideration allows the patient to proceed exploring his awareness, a quality of free associating develops. I had not instructed any such rule; it is his spontaneous discovery and creation. Good, freeing feelings seem to accompany this process, and he starts to make connections which constitute beginnings of narratives to explain the ideas and feelings which prompted his decision to seek psychotherapy. These steps seem to me to be indigenous to his self reparative interests. The patient may feel free to select from our empathic offerings with a minimum of imposed, iatrogenic transference reactions.

Just as Anna O. and then Emmy von N. invented the free association principle, especially the latter's requesting Freud "not to keep on asking her where this and that came from, but to let her tell me what she had to say," I aim to let each patient construct and modify his own methods for proceeding and see him revising and selecting from the array of stereotypical classical techniques. Ideally, each patient will reinvent the psychoanalytic ways suiting his deep search as I negotiate the good enough, safe atmosphere and liberate the fuller awareness which leads to spontaneous reconstructions and narratives to give felt meaning to the painful affect and the constraining compromises in their defense mechanisms. So also, in principle, each patient rediscovers and recovers those aspects of psychoanalytic theory which affect him and effect meaningful repairs of one's personhood, self and relating. If we listen well enough we will perceive new hypotheses being glimpsed and perhaps developed in the client's bold or brave extensions into realms beyond our reigning theories. Two such rewarding experiences were reported in detail in a joint 1953 article (Coleman and Shor) and the fresh theoretical approach was suggested in my 1963 presentation to the British Psychoanalytic Society under the theme "Self-Provocation and Reparation." (See Chapter XI).

The absence of response or interest from my colleagues at that time moved me to identify with the boldness of my patients and I developed the hypotheses further in the course of five years as a research associate on a project for a psychoanalytic theory of action at the Southern California Psychoanalytic Institute. My contribution there was published in 1972 under the ambitious title, "Two Principles of Reparative Regression: Self-Traumatization and Self-Provocation." It proved to be another setback for these ideas; in the seventeen years since then I've seen not one reference, friendly or critical, to that publication. I began to realize that a more careful and slower expression of the viewpoint was necessary, and perhaps with more clinical detail, as I am attempting here.

It may be in describing how I formulate my interpretations of the transferences that I can reach some bridges to the classical tradition which I had found so nourishing for nearly twenty years. I assume that at the core of all transferences is an uncertainty, a doubt whether the therapist will respond to favor the patient's good development or will be an obstruction in old or new ways. The expression of transferences is thus in part a test of the therapentic relationship, a part that is crucial for the alliance. My recent emphasis is on the negotiating a safe working relationship and then the deepending of the patient's search for his own reparative intents through very careful empathy; some successes in these preliminary phases must precede any venturing any psycho-dynamic interpretations.

Then I proceed, in a style of gentle persistence, to comment on hidden complaints, doubts and desires.

Instead of exposing self-deceptions or resistances I note the mixed feelings in the ambivalences I sense in his transference projections. The friendly manner may allow the patient to recover his unconscious intent to test the working alliance for my hidden attitudes and his readiness to explore his conflicts and fantasy-laden wishes. My easy repetitions of such themes may eventually register and echo his hidden hopes as he persists in testing me with his armory of defense mechanisms. If we survive as an alliance, he can experience the new greater strength of his primary wish to repair and thus be free of a dependence on magical gestures or a submission to a presumptive, if benign, authority in the therapist.

Then we can proceed to develop his narratives as far as *he* wants. We can refine and revise our understandings to his satisfaction. We play together. More moments of merging are experienced and he can openly enjoy the occasions of fusion feelings yet feel free to make selective identifications which equip him with "transmuting internalizations" (Kohut, 1977). He may feel himself to be a changed person and even thank me.

What the patient has taken in he must yet assimilate as his own and proceed with internalized models to employ in self analysis as life may precipitate a felt need. Though he may decide to come back for more joint work (Freud's "Analysis Interminable,") he reports feeling ready to risk more, be more in charge as the agent in future dilemmas.

Permit me to quote the parting words of the first patient who helped move me to this way of practicing therapy, in 1953, soon after I met Balint's writings. The patient expressed surprise at discovering and relishing feelings vaguely familiar: "I never knew I had such good feelings, never knew I could have them; and they're mine. . . . You were such a nice baby sitter for me" (Shor, 1954). Balint had described that "temporary illusion" of completely harmonious love as "primary love." We later developed the image into "primary illusion" (Shor and Sanville, 1978) as a dialectic spiral of separate self and relating.

As the patient moves to terminate or even just to try taking a pause in our joint work for testing himself on his own, I remind myself that there are inequalities and differences between us, so it will not be maintained as a fully mutual dialogue between equals. Therefore I remain ready to recognize and accept what claims he makes for an independent status, including silences, intermissions and terminations of our dialogue, our work together. I also show, when necessary, that I expect him to respect the privacy, the autonomy and the self-responsibility I may claim for myself. I imply or state that I hope our joint consideration of his puzzles and pains may yield him new ways of experiencing aspects of his difficulties, some of which may yet be hidden from us both. En route, I've tried to make my side of the dialogue as free of instructions as possible, whether about the frequency of sessions, the proper procedures for our sessions, the regularity of our meetings or the emphasis on specific themes of content or interpretation. My private expectation and hope continue that he will increase his active responsibility for measuring his readiness to claim enough independence to venture his private self-analysis and management of his ongoing developmental wishes and potentialities—that he become his own analyst. I say that I remain open to his return, if he chooses. I never "terminate"; Pedder agrees that the very term is "inappropriate" (1988, p. 504).

This ethic is not spelled out by Freud or by our classical tradition. I am proposing a more detailed implementation of it in our work for its therapeutic values. I see some possible movement in this direction. For example, P. Dewald (1972, pp. 305-6), in his official GAP report, alerted us to the need to relax our demands for precision in "the formidable problems of accuracy, measurement of possible distortions, and research design involved in such assessments" and to allow that " . . . decisions in technique, such as the timing or content of an interpretation, imply that the analyst has recognized . . . that the patient can now accept and appreciate his understanding of the material." I hear a fresh sensitivity to the patient's measuring and directing his aims in therapy and in living.

Instead of precision in our definitions and theories, I speak for the therapist's careful, self aware concern about the qualities of his presence and his responsibility for refining his readiness to attend, in modesty, offering the special forms of working, loving and playing which are my definition of the practice of psychoanalytic therapy. The qualities of experience which most characterize the favorable therapeutic process are reflective autonomy and responsive intimacy in both participants in the dialogue.

The growing influences from Winnicott and Balint in these directions are becoming very evident, as in the edited volume by Fromm and Smith (1989). For example, Fromm favors André Green's thesis for the "nondirective availability" (p. 464) of the analyst, though he warns that it "generates anxiety and must be repeatedly tested, warded off, or otherwise negotiated" (ibid). Such wariness may derive from his traditional position that "the rules or frame are set by the analyst" (ibid). Rather than indulge the anxious patient with this benign authoritarianism, I have suggested full and flexible negotiating from the start, and then more sensitive empathizing in depth to fortify the latent autonomy for a stronger working alliance. Feeling in charge, the patient will manage the pace and choose to invite our interpretations. Yet we must ask what may help the analyst to tolerate the greater openness and flexibility which I am recommending; this is the issue in the next chapter.

VI

Therapist Experiencing

How patient can one be and at what costs? Having termed the
making of hypotheses, interpretations, and narratives as forms
of play which both patient and analyst may best come to do
together, with the patient leading the way, I must recognize
the necessary presence also of elements of work and love in
the freewheeling that renders the play deeply affective and effective. Working and loving at the other's behest are not pure
joy. And if the therapist's experiencing were totally interac-
tional, his involvement would be predominantly accommodating and following, and would become extremely draining and
dehumanizing unless he had the infinite patience and alertness
of the most abundant and generous god. A day's labor would
require continuous lending one's self, with ever flexible sensitiveness, to unpredictable series of responding experiences:
meeting the varied complex calls and rejections, compromising
in unconsciously subtle negotiations, empathizing in fitting attunements, identifying and sorting transference tests and cau-
tious invitations to intervene, respecting pace, privacy and
autonomy and reserving one's even correct insights in patient
silence.

Such active abstinence with minimum initiative would be
unbearable without some balancing, even compensatory asser-

tions of my own, mostly in my private silence and sometimes bits of open self expression, even self indulgence. These excursions are not only necessary, I find, but they may, in careful doses, enrich the therapeutic values for the experiencing patient. He can notice my actual limitations for his absolute wishes in the primary illusion and he will learn to measure his tolerance for my deficiencies.

That ultimate fantasy for a perfect resonance, when revived and felt, can provide the motivation and model for beginning new efforts in repairing, reconstructing and creating better ways and better equipment for making his life more rewarding. In that process, the patient may entertain, educate, illuminate and inspire me to rethink my own patterns of living—working, loving and playing. But such benefits keep me essentially *reacting* in our actual exchanges until our therapeutic alliance has developed to the safe freedoms of playing together in producing new meanings and understandings. Then I feel ready to use myself more actively and with some initiative. My free play will be rooted in my capacities and maturities for that ideal dialogue which essentially equal persons can conduct. Under the earned circumstances of balanced mutual dialogue, we are no longer therapist and patient and he soon would feel "ready to proceed with self-analysis . . . free to choose, to create, more realistic, more rewarding celebrations" (Shor, 1954).

When the patient disappears, my residue of unfinished needs to assert, to dialogue, to play become my separate burden, responsibility and opportunity. After all the accommodating, we too must make our assimilations into the texture of our lives, actual and potential. All along we may have been reviewing, mostly privately, our errors and our successful responses, our failings and our good effectivenesses. We seal specific aspects of the course of professional experiences with some mourning for the patient. Despite the regrets, some glowings of delight and perhaps of ennervating pride, the closures are not final. We store the faulty edges and the unfitted deposits on the infinite shelves of our unconsciously eternal selves mixed in with some precious pearls and luminescent bits. These reserves need not stay on the shelves. They can be moved later to enter into a variety of functions and contexts, professional and personal, and make for significant changes in self expression and in other dialogues.

Before and beyond the active changing that may develop from our experiencing psychotherapy as therapists there are the more elaborate and less overt forms of action (Schaffer 1976). These private qualities of experiencing inner being and becoming comprehend the reflecting and imagining which surround our participating with the patient, though they may or may not have entered into the therapeutic process. Those awarenesses which were expressed surely modify the interplay, hopefully towards the patient's objective, and their energies may be felt to be discharged. Those which are not given expression remain in our private reservoirs in more loose and fragmented states. Unconscious linkings occur and can render them ready for our evolving reflections, our purposes, for our sakes, for our personhood.

Each form and phase of our clinical functioning can foster a particular sifting of our relevant resources—such as when we are called on to accept a fresh consultation: I review my wishes and needs for another patient, my readiness emotionally and practically to rearrange my schedules, my confidences and convictions about my theories and ways in practicing. The endless illustrations possible here are all to palpable. My prompting of more self consciousness in these obvious situations may favor the continual rethinking of one's theoretical and ethical assumptions in practice as well as one's styles of role playing. For example, how do we anticipate beginning a session or greeting a new person? The "ethical" clinician can advance the position of the humanistic philosopher:

> In *I and Thou*, Martin Buber invites us to delight in the spiritual processes of initiating every relationship, even every genuine human contact: "All actual life is encounter." Buber has enriched the existential stance with a forward moving optimism about the potential senses of discovery and growth in open inter-acting. He recognizes the hope "to be embraced" in moments of intimate meeting as deriving from the model of "some paradise in the primary age of human-

72

ity" [Balint's Primary Love?]. . . . From our view of the on-going phases of development, we see a necessary supplement to the creative drive toward sensitive meetings. Equally essential is the complementary process of creative separating. Thus our dialectic may be: "All true living is meeting and parting." Each step in fuller relating permits a richer separating and autonomy, which then fosters a better next relating. The spiral dialectic can go on either within the same relationship or in the next relationships, throughout all the phases of human growth and development (Model of the Primary Illusion, Shor and Sanville, 1978, pp. 110-111).

An anecdote comes to mind. After the Tavistock years (1961-64) I left for Los Angeles with a transitional arrangement to do research at a California State Hospital for the severely retarded. During orientation there, I was shown some very extreme cases, literally basket cases, of gross globs of protoplasm in grotesque shapes, yet with some features and signs of organismic life. Facing one such "person" fretting and quivering, I looked to its eye-like organs in a global head of a sort. I slowly nodded my head, with a smile, as Spitz had done decades before in his work with healthy infants. The somebody inside the distorted mass of protoplasm seemed to stop its agitated shaking, direct its "eyes" to me, and seemed to do a nod back to me. The regular staff of the hospital smiled tolerantly, but silently, as I hypothesized afterward about the social exchange of greeting I had experienced.

I have no follow-up data on possible mourning reactions for my having left that unusual self perhaps abruptly. However, in subsequent weeks, when those musical Beatles reached great popularity in the U.S. and their recordings were piped into the hospital wards, the staff did see and wonder at the change of behavior for many severely primitive patients. Some who had been curled in the corner, completely incontinent and yet able to extrude their intestines through anal muscular manipulations, these patients, on hearing enough of the new Beatles' rhythms and tones, stopped their self manipulations and did rock their entire bodies to the rhythms, perhaps feeling met in particularly penetrating ways.

73

My past professional experience did not prepare me to work directly with these severe patients, but I did begin some research with the hospital attendants to learn how they sometimes manages to stay on in such challenging positions for years. The cue I found was the way an attendant would "adopt" one patient as her child needing great love and care, but then to perform duties with other patients in a mechanized, depersonalized spirit. We each have our limits to empathy which may allow genuinely open greetings.

Here is the *possibility* of receiving the patient, each time, with a willingness for the dialogue processes to emerge. Bion has recommended we enter the session "with no memory, no desire" (1964 and 1977) but an openness to the unexpected and the unpredictable. Reik's whole book (1937) heralds the readiness for surprise in psychoanalytic therapy. Even Erikson's still valuable basic perspective, with its "eight ages" and the "schedule of virtues" (1950 and 1964) was recently reopened by him to convert that eighth stage from "integrity" and "renunciation . . . in wisdom" to a freer, more play-full spirit of seeking the unforseeable and the unknowable. The greater our sense of potential supplies, the wider our search for self expression, the higher our reach in exchange and dialogue, the richer and rounder the spiral of experiencing. To approach the patient with these anticipations will surely influence the therapist's ways of practice in detail.

How precisely is such influence affecting one's patience? What are the variables? The store of residues from practice, even the most correct and ethical conducting of psychotherapy, will call for new opportunities to generate dialogue within and without the professional context. The natural and necessary respect for privacy among colleagues has thwarted our understanding of the personal equation in effecting successful work. Gossip and more subtle retributions have been meted out to those who have tried to raise such considerations in any direct expressions of hypotheses. We remember Freud's shyness in this direction, even in his eighties. He does hint that "among the factors which influence the prospects of analytic treatment and add to its difficulties . . . in the same manner as the resistances, must be reckoned not only the nature of the patient's ego but the individuality of the analyst" (1937, p. 247). He here assigns to Ferenczi the responsibility of pronouncing concern with "the analyst's having learnt sufficiently from his own errors and mistakes and having got the better of the weak points of his personality." And soon after Ferenczi dared, Freud held him at a distance. Who will bell the cat?

Many of us do deliver our critiques and suggestions for these private issues concealed within our publications on the abstract, theoretical and methodological level. Conflicting schools of thought arise, some less cultish than others. Training institutes split and tighten control over loyal followers. But perhaps these ways show our limits to the play and dialogue we can afford or risk. Freud early put Adler and Jung out in order to protect the safe space he wished for proceeding with developing his beginnings for psychoanalysis. Does my definition of play become useless when I call my theoretical formulations playful expressions of the residues from the fuller and primary experience of psychotherapy in practice?

There are certain models for my giving clear priority to the clinical experiencing. I remember my year as a supervisee, in 1950-51, with Ludwig Jekels, a formally ordained member of the orthodox New York Psychoanalytic Society yet who seemed to have succeeded in keeping his distance from the constraints and cliques of that conservative group. He came to Freud's psychoanalysis very early, actually older than Freud, worked his own paths with a privateness that yielded fewer than 200 pages, in all, of publications in the field, none of it polemical, from over fifty years of practice. He did much teaching and training and he did explore new ideas outside the pale of his Society. But he maintained an essentially non-public, non-doctrinal position. Each of his very few articles weaves original themes through the currently lively concepts and controversies in the the field. For example, for the theoretical problems of aggression, guilt and the death principle, he offered the working hypotheses that : Work provides not only the most important and socially approved opportunity for the discharge of aggression. It also prevents guilt [and] provides narcissistic gratification . . . whether through the social need for the product or the appreciation for their achievement . . . the worker is confirmed, as it were, in his omnipotence. (1952, p.86). This approach clearly stimulated the reparative theme in my thinking.

Jekels was in his early nineties when he agreed to supervise me, without an institutional framework. I recall his alert and sharp attention and comments to the clinical details I presented. He speculated and reflected with vitality; he played in private and remained free in his personhood (Shor, 1953a). I know hardly anything personal about him and have not sought to learn the inside story. He managed to avert the invasions of privacy which to this day dog Freud and other well published analysts. Public play may be dangerous to your mental health even when you do not put a precious premium on your abstract theoretical products. Freud frankly speculated, often calling his work "as if" stories, and he also warns us not to give out biographical data in any detail (Shor, 1961).

What a dilemma for our theme of the influence of the personal character and ethics on the way one does psychotherapy! Following Ferenczi as his prime teacher, Balint made several allusions over the years in his publications to this linking of personal maturity and the styles of practice. There is some evidence that the recent two decades have shown more open mentions of countertransference problems and the real relationship factors, beyond the traditional, formal consideration of correct theories and 'proper technique' which remain the displaced battlegrounds for contending viewpoints about method and ethics. Perhaps we are freeing ourselves, some of us, from an earnest concentration on intellectual precision for the multi-layered data we are experiencing in our work which is so rooted in hardly verbalizable cues and clues to inner sensing and awareness. We are spending greater effort, for well over a decade, in formulations about the nature of language expression in development, with the burgeoning studies of linguistics and narratives. I think we need to refine those residues from internal reflecting and unfinished dialoguing; play is not a belittling term in the psychic economy and structure but it need not be confused with love and work. Every gain from discursive play can be assimilated, saving time and energy for the next turn in the dialectical spiral, for next forms and areas of exploration and invention.

I will tell this story perhaps at some risk, which I think I can afford now at age seventy. At age fifteen I found my way to a burlesque theatre in the Bowery of New York City to see and learn more about how adults presented sexuality. Each stage show, about one hour in length, consisted of several, perhaps five or six, acts with jazzy comedians and undressing or partially undressed females. One of these episodes remains memorable. A young man at the threshold of frankly adult sex, about age 20, in that more puritanical period, earnestly appealed to a suave roué with much experience, to tell how he has succeeded in seducing the girls. The boasting rake gave accounts, with song and dance, of the persuasive devices and maneuvers he had exercised in his successful exploits. He told of the many "lines" he spoke to trick the naive females into his carnal clutches. The young man listened to him with awe and looked breathlessly at the parade of nearly nude figures behind the gauzy curtain. But then he stopped and seemed to recover his own home grounds, his preferred ethics, and asked the bragging scoundrel: "But what if you really love the girl? What do you say then?" To his credit, the middle aged man slowed down and softened and said simply, "Oh then, you just touch her hand gently, look right into her eyes, and you don't have to say a darn thing." And the little orchestra burst into a loud tune of celebration to the applause of the audience.

I also remember that, between the hourly stage shows, the theatre presented lovely nature films, mostly of plants and animals developing and lounging in settings of lyrical peace and abundance. To this day, a very favorite hobby is watching nature films showing the amazing variety and details of adaptations in evolution. Both parts of the presentation, the Burlesque and the Educational films, seemed to advance images of primary harmony as basic models in nature. Within a year I changed my high school interest in math and physics to the goal of life work in psychoanalysis.

I am not proposing a lazy, indolent indifference to theoretical formulations; we do need that fun to nourish advances in our practice, but we can hold our hypotheses more lightly and flexibly so that more of the subjective data may find a place in the net of our anticipations and reflections, perhaps even to illuminate and vitalize the stricter structures. Formal theory aims to provide a context, a safe space, but the experiencing must be open to the unidentified and the unexpected.

This seemingly anti-intellectual stand needs support wherever it can find it. From the halls of official tradition, Kurt Eissler comes forward with a bold study of *Medical Orthodoxy and the Future of Psychoanalysis* (1965) to admit that "it will have become evident that, when an analyst reports his findings, they cannot be accepted on faith . . . " and he finally concludes that "All this leads me to believe that analysts should devote their primary attention to the elaboration of the psychoanalytic technique . . . " (p. 389). Concerned about hard words with a manipulative tone, I would translate "technique" into a sense of method or approach in work with the patient; the change would encourage more attention to the subjective ethics in our experiencing the therapeutic relating.

Precise verbal formulations are necessary for technological operations, which can provide a safer space for the love and play which may follow that first work in psychotherapy, the negotiations, which does offer models and promises for a basic security to the wary person. The therapist needs to protect himself too; he will likely know better than the patient, caught in his problems, that flexibility in negotiating will help to bridge the gaps in making changes. Here is his greatest labor, to offer compromises which permit both participants to consider and reconsider the arrangements as they influence the not-yet-conscious interests affected. A spirit of tentativeness softens the agreements. The most frequent phrase I use in this early phase is "Let's try and see how it goes." This note is given for all manner of details, whether the frequency of sessions, the use of the couch, the taking of a break or terminating. The initiative of the patient should be given priority in negotiating a compromise or a trail period. In this way, we are inviting the patient to lead in the evaluation of every aspect; he can reach for as much precision as he seeks, and change his mind. Exactitude in subjective experience is a private measurement. We are responsible for providing the atmosphere for his reflections and judgments, to the depths and measures he chooses. "The business of analysis is to secure the best possible conditions for the functioning of the ego" (Freud, XXIII, p. 250).

That right for the therapist to protect himself, his interests, his plans and potentialities, can be the hiding place for pathological influences on the patient, of course. Our society provides defenses against such possibilities as our culture claims more civil rights for self responsibility and equips the populace to know more about experts' behaviors and assumptions.

Public protests and critiques of psychoanalysts are rife today at most levels of educational maturity, from the sophisticated *New Yorker* magazine to the how-to-paperbacks all about us. The proliferation of self help and peer therapy groups is a most constructive trend for our general advancement of mental health; these movements apply and refine the ideas proposed by the professionals, just as within the most sensitive analytic process. Cynical debunking of these popular efforts is no more helpful than are the subtle authoritarian presumptions and professional debunking which secretly continue in the private therapeutic sessions. The "layman's" explorations and criticisms are significant cues to stimulate advances for the specialized practitioner. I welcome the bold note in the work of A. Lazare, who wrote "The Customer Approach to Psychotherapy" (1975).

Our work in first negotiating will surely be tested in ways unique to each patient. We call these tests transference reactions or distortions. Rather than rushing to interpret them, I repeat my negotiations and make the flexible compromises I can afford, and say so. My persistence in abstaining from giving my interpretive hypotheses "can become a useful weapon against his neurotic obstinance and a model for the greater sense of his own abundance" (Shor, 1954). The emergence of the working alliance from the negotiating prepares for the unifying closeness that develops with the resonating empathy we offer carefully, and, again, flexibly. If our hints about reparative intents help to deepen the patient's experience of his affective complaining and desiring, he comes to call on us to suggest new answers, new understandings for his own failures. Then, invited, we begin to play by making interpretations which are anchored in the actual transference manifestations before us. Working to refine and revise these interventions, we, together, begin to construct the narratives he seeks, to own his personhood in perspectives. We remain available to his pacing. We wait, ready for his decision to terminate, or to return.

The high-mindedness of that model of patient therapeutic practice needs some further grounding. Ideal images are at best long range goals, or even just cues toward next possibilities. General moralistic slogans about failures make for resentment or depression, of course. Therapists' confessions about personal errors are palliative and undermining, like reassurances and excusings, to the patient in pain. What may be useful are indications and illustrations of reparative intents and efforts which serve to renew the search for better arrangements, autoplastic and alloplastic at the same time. To illustrate, I do not ever discuss my patients in any identifiable way but I am willing to give selective, screened accounts of myself to demonstrate the principles being proposed. I risk such exposure here; the possibly controversial exchange raises questions about sharing reasonable and useful respect to the patient.

Many years ago, in the midst of my divorce process, I found myself too preoccupied to do my work properly. I felt I had to reduce my schedule and do more personal reflection and management. I did gradually claim my private preferences to work fewer hours and when asked directly I said I had to take care of some things, nothing more. When asked indirectly, in symbolic ways, I look up puzzled and note the transferential signs of uneasy and other feelings which block a simple direct question. I do not respond with any content about the reasons for my preferences or scheduling unless and until the patient, at another occasion, can ask me with easy directness about my suggestion that I would like to change any arrangements; then we are both ready to negotiate details.

One patient, a candidate in our Institute, who apparently felt well advanced in his self regulated analysis, went further. From the currents of information likely to flow in and around the membership of our professional society, he learned of my marital disruption in progress and confronted me roughly as follows (I never make or keep notes on the specific statements of any identifiable patient person):

> You've got me worried. If you have serious troubles in your personal relationships, why should I trust you to know how to help me understand my problems with my wife? I think I have a right to ask you what's going on in your life. What's it all about?

I responded essentially agreeing with his right but then said I was willing to reply with some thoughts about the qualities of relationship *I* felt to be missing or badly distorted, and about my having made several kinds of efforts to remedy and repair the relating to my deeper satisfactions, and about my hopes to recover my willingness, in time, for renewing my search for a better relationship. I stated in advance that I would not discuss or speculate about the attitudes or behaviors of my wife. He said, "Okay; let's hear the story." I began to tell, as I promised, my growing awareness of disaffections and bad feelings, about which I had reflected, with private pain. I paused often these first five or seven minutes as a punctuation marker, like a period, or at least a semicolon. He intervened to say in sum: "That' enough. Let's get back to me. If I find such difficulties in my life, I'd like to be able to deal with it as you are, if the dynamics fit my situation." And he proceeded to free associate about the edges and elements of concern for himself which felt unanchored. He had been preparing himself to decide about terminating the analysis and resumed exploring this possible choice.

By not taking notes, or recordings, I may be subject to an accusation that I've reconstructed the facts and idealized the event. I cannot satisfy such a charge and I ask only that the principles of method here illustrated be considered as part of a general approach to patients choosing us as assistants. To platter the points, because I think them crucial, I did respect the patient's direct expressions of his rights to be in charge, to assert them forthrightly yet flexibly, and yet I protected my personal privacy while sharing specific assumptions of values in human relating.

One's ethics, in the ongoing development toward a fuller maturity and personhood, are always influencing how we practice. A good enough working alliance may come to earn and deserve our responding in principle to the patient's inquiries with a strength and sensitivity that surely is considerate and confirming to his goals for himself, as well as mine. This level of dialogue can be especially appropriate when he is near deciding to terminate the analysis, at least for the present.

VII

Work, Love and Play

However ethical the therapist may be in his practice, properly mannered, considerate, comfortably responsive, fully attending and patient, he surely needs to transcend the neutral *laissez-faire* qualities in his stance for his own psychic economy. He has worked: negotiating, helping to construct explanations, develop hypotheses and create narratives from the data, the behavior and expressions of the patient. Stimulated by spontaneous empathies and by the armory of theories in his professional training and later reading, the therapist experiences far more than the classical blank screen or mirror stereotype suggests. Even as we prune that literature and our complex private identifications and countertransferences, a substantial residue of internal reactions remains within our responsiveness to the overt behavior and unconscious dynamics of the patient. If we have held our positions lightly and flexibly, waited to be invited by the client who feels himself in charge of our pace of active participation and we have expressed ourselves tentatively, as auxiliary observers and friendly allies, then our heritage and reservoir of theories, hypotheses, hunches, guesses and impressions may become more useful to the client's reflective considerations and conscious testings.

Since transference observations and interpretations remain "the main instrument" (Freud, 1914) to guide our empathy and implement our suggested explanatory narratives, this approach may "call itself psychoanalysis, even though it arrives at results other than my own" (Freud, *idem.*). We know how Freud modified basic hypotheses as he gained clinical experience and observed the changing social and cultural variables. So far biology and chemistry are producing data not yet applicable to the subtleties we evoke, or imagine, in our client's reaching for analytic help. Experienced patients continuing their search for fulfillments, privately defined and measured, are provoking a rethinking of the processes and criteria for goals in living and their achievement; and the current professional literature seems less interested in setting up criteria for cure or for judging suitability of patients for psychoanalytic therapy. We are opening our gates and now need to expand our approaches. The basic ethics of psychoanalysis become more relevant to everyone, experienced patients all of us.

Perhaps we can be bolder in approaching again some general concepts for the recurrently honored and sometimes rejected doctrine of the psychic unity of all humanity. I propose that every person seeks fulfillment in three types of functions: work, love and play. Those new studies of interactions in infancy may be equipping us to recognize certain early strivings as more universal, ultimately helpful toward one harmonious world, freer of constraints from class, caste, race, sex or creed. The revolutions are spreading with louder clamors for so far unavailable entitlements, despite the greater felt dangers to us all from these rising expectations. The outcomes are less predictable today, just as we begin our depth psychoanalytic efforts with less certainty or precision about objectives and outcomes. Yet some tenets of a doctrine of psychic unity of humanity remain necessary to support the experiencing of empathy and interpretation. However partial the communality, the overlap, here is where consensus and dialogue find roots to grow toward an identicality, which may be my most controversial hypothesis about ultimate human motivation. Perhaps the freest liberation experience may best move us closer to that imagined model; yet some kind of instinct or drive theory is necessary, I think, as opening gambits.

I personally cannot afford extreme positions like absolute anarchism or total ethical relativism in my anticipations about human desires and goals, much as I may try to approach and hold those stances in my work with the analytic process. And even when I succeed in convincing the client of my intent of ethical neutrality, especially at sensitive and crucial moments of negotiation in our dialogue relationship, I protect my economy with the principle that his freely chosen value decisions are his separate right and responsibility and not necessarily my preferences. My views remain in my private province. Probably my inner convictions do leak at times, and are caught by his unconscious perceptions and projections. I do look out for such subtle slips between us and restate my primary interest in serving him to pursue his own models and ends. Such exchanges do serve to decrease his projections of final authority on to me and make it easier to be and work with him in my preferred style. Such events also keep me more open to learn new ways of experiencing human dilemmas, for my work with him and with myself. Perhaps I become better able to afford the liberating generosity which does characterize my criteria for profound psychoanalytic psychotherapy.

And yet I do listen for confirmations of my current models and goals in life, and my perceptions may selectively influence my interventions, my negotiations, empathies and interpretations. So I will try to formulate here my present perspectives about ultimate goals and models with a hope that such self-expression will foster further dialogues, both internal reflections and exchanges with the other, the "objects" (that unfortunate analytic term for persons valued). The more I experience such dialogue processes the less likely will my listening be rigid or distorted and the more likely may I rethink and revise current convictions.

Here I confess or boast that my concern with formulating about ultimate aims in psychotherapy and the criteria for mental health began very early and my major writings over the decades were all renewed approaches to these issues as my training and experience developed. The first attempt was a substantial individual research project entitled "Problems in Defining Adjustment," in 1938 as an undergraduate, while an intern in training in the University Clinic. My Master's thesis three years later expanded and sharpened the theme to "Criteria for Defining Adjustment." The first two years of my formal analytic training preceeded my doctoral dissertation, which was 225 pages on *Changing Objectives in Psychological Treatment*, in 1948; this was researched and written while I did psychotherapy as an Instructor at Yale University. Since that unpublished dissertation attempts a psycho-social perspective about the historical emergence of psychoanalytic levels of approaching the person, I have placed some pages of its summary formulations in a later chapter, on psychotherapy without diagnostic labels.

What may be new are my present hypotheses about the correspondence between the therapist's ethical phases of method and the ultimate goals in our patients. I am proposing that what all clients seek at their most basic levels of analyzed clarity, are improvements in their readiness for work, love and play. And these are the functions which the analyst can and should offer as qualities of his participation. This approach contains a particular sequence of qualities of working together, loving and playing together. The forms of practice and the contents in psychotherapeutic dialogue are expressions of the same three themes in human complaining and desiring; the ingredients and the atmosphere can be resonant and consonant in quality. The patient can experience a coherence of words and style, of form and content of relating. Such parallel connecting may be especially integrating while also liberating for the private self as well as for the rewards of human merging and exchange.

My aim is to identify the natural sequence, work, love and play, in our patient's experience; yet, since, in early benign infancy states the three processes are closely interwoven we might find, at any phase of psychotherapy, some impulses and expressions of all three qualities as we recognize the predominance of a primary one. The ratios are unpredictable so we must move slowly and flexibly; therefore the emphasis is on patience.

First is the work of sensitive negotiating and flexible accommodating for developing that safe space which both respects mutual autonomies and favors a sense of sharing the tasks ahead. The yield is the richer data of both malignant and benign fantasies long buried in the aborted complaining and desiring which create the relationship. I remind you of my earlier assumption which supports, guides and motivates the negotiating work of psychotherapy: the primary model of a dialogue in the newborn and the resulting dialectical spiral in growth and development.

The elemental nature of the exchanges between early infant and caretaker encourages us to make persisting efforts for discovering ways to establish contact with ever more primitive patients, as we fortify ourselves with richer, private cohesion and flexibility. Work with "psychotic states" seems to me most challenging in this sense; so also do I find psychotherapy with children as difficult. I recognize that my practice, primarily with self supporting adult patients in voluntary analysis, has made it easier to explore the approach I describe and to experience the ethical attitudes being advanced. Braver therapists may feel ready to venture these principles with the more severely dependent and damaged persons; the degrees and types of clinical inventiveness must be greatly expanded.

With my fuller person-patients, I have risked and made errors which derailed our dialogues (Spitz, 1964) often. It was reassuring to read Winnicott's public apology for beginning too soon to play at his own pace:

> It appals me to think how much deep change I have prevented and delayed in patients in a certain classification category by my personal need to interpret. If only we can wait, the patient arrives at understanding creatively and with immense joy and now I enjoy this joy more than I need the sense of having been clever. . . . I think I interpret mainly to let the patient know the limits of my understanding. The

principle is that it is the patient and only the patient who has the answers. We may or may not enable him or her to encompass what is known or become aware of it with acceptance (1968, p. 25).

In this work, Winnicott also identifies core ethical cues to the approach of that British Independent Tradition (Kohon, 1985):

We are poor indeed if we are only sane (p. 161). Richness of quality rather than health (absence of illness) is at the top of the ladder of human progress (p. 173).

A special note of interest in this perspective is the quality of openness for the work of therapy; it is less a task to be accomplished, more of a dialogue between ever growing companions who come to feel attunements, resonance and unifying agreements in empathy. In this spirit certain human elements, like a simple friendliness, are likely to emerge, but when the dialogue is derailed a fresh effort at more careful negotiating can rerail this friendly process.

The meaning of empathy has begun to be diffused from loose over-use recently, especially by the Self psychologists, in a burgeoning literature. My meanings for the word are here contained within the experiences of that gradual attuning, resonating and also consenting to agreeable silences and comfortable separating. The special proviso in my view is that the patient's lead is regularly confirmed; he is in charge. Thus it is not a mutual love between equal persons; it leaves a larger element of work in the therapist's experiencing while negotiating and empathizing. The patient's payments signify that he has done his work before the session and therefore is justified in dominating the proceedings. His labor may have been to deal with his relationships to the parent or mate who is actually providing the money; these dealings do imply compromises with his own personhood. Therefore I regularly hand the bill to the patient and if he does not hand the payment to me directly, I look for signs of self compromising in his dependent attitudes in his negotiating with me. In principle, this approach may prove useful even with children. However he has paid for the hour, he is entitled to be insistent about aiming to gain his lost functions and his hope to gather them into a rewarding long-time investment, while the therapist works to find right points and levels of contact (Havens, 1986).

The patient may enjoy the loving empathy but the therapist is charged, I think, to help him to know and feel his discontents and also to recover his inherent wishes for a separate self functioning, with his own resources. The therapist's heavier labor should move him to move the patient on beyond empathy. I remember well that nicely advancing patient who asked me to be quiet while he explored his mood and developed hypotheses at his pace.

Friends and family relatives have sometimes asked my opinion about the competence of the analyst whom they are considering or seeing. I do not express a judgment about the subject, not only because I cannot know the actual dynamics of the therapeutic relationship but also because the inquirer's question implies a feeling of double bind or compromise. Rather do I, in all cases, say simply that there seems to be an uncertainty about being met which has not been fully expressed to the analyst in question and that a thorough exploring of such doubts can be the most helpful pathway for the patient to gain more of what he is seeking from the therapy. I recommend to the inquirer a direct confrontation, a complaining to his heart's discontent, and then awaiting a response which leads to some of the personal insight and emotional benefits for which he initially sought treatment. If his first challenges do not yield satisfactory understandings, and seem to be mostly a defensive response from that therapist, I encourage a further discussion of the doubts with a requirement that the dialogue will yield something more of what the patient is trying to know about himself.

I privately anticipate that the patient's focused complaining may help the therapist see the neglected theme and be helped to get on with his proper work with the patient. I summarize my perspective about the doubt at hand by proposing that the inquiring patient should try to sharpen his judgment about the usefulness of the therapeutic engagement and express more fully the texture of his feelings and desires for himself. To paraphrase my view, love is not enough for the whole person. Beyond empathy there is private play with its permeating component of free, flexible autonomy.

That term, play, has become more difficult to define than any other I have been advancing. I limit myself to those meanings intrinsic and central to the process of psychoanalysis that I am here trying to delineate, the playfulness inherent in the developing of satisfying narratives about one's development, the inventiveness in constructing hypotheses and the fun in testing them in and out of session. I also mean the experience of timeless reflecting on one's possibilities in living. The patient may or may not share these processes with the therapist but I think that some sharing will facilitate the therapist's confluent playing and thus create more of a spirit of equality. When both play together, the inequalities in the previous work and the somewhat biased loving which gave the patient priority may both be transcended and the more equal exchanging in joint play favors a more liberating and selective internalizing by the patient of the functions modeled by the analyst as analyst. Unresolved transferences are less likely to persist and he is freer to move out into more living as his own person with an enhanced, better equipped identity. He can better regulate his work, love and play to experience and discover satisfactions, both long desired and perhaps previously not anticipated. In the terms of an earlier decade:

> Repossessed, with the conscious insights worked through, with his wish for the primary and ultimate give and take, the patient can come to a valid decision to terminate analysis. Equipped with this knowledge, in experience, he is ready to proceed with self-analysis. He and she become free, to choose, to create, more realistic, more rewarding celebrations. (Shor, 1954, p. 32).

My schematic formula of work, love, then play may sound artificial, an imposed, contrived plan. There are these dangers. Balint has described the "ocnophilic" and "philobotic" biases

(1959) in psychotherapy; the therapist may be fostering submissive dependences (ocnophilia) when he is "too" protective and regulating, or forcing heroics (philobatism) when the therapist is too provocatively silent and unexpressive. Iatrogenic transferences result, but when the analyst corrects his mismeasure of the patient's readiness and responds to a question or invitation, there is a piece of relief, a return to home grounds. Such rerailing of the dialogue spiral is a delicate job of repairing a wasteful and unfortunate experience; yet both persons may learn from the errors and feel a bond in grieving together. These rerailing spirals occur as subtle combinations of work, love and play together. Some occasions of failure in the dialogue are inevitable from the unpredictable differences in pace of feeling, recognition and expression. Human variability has deeper sources than specific complaints and desires. Leaving aside, with some sense of apology, for now, much of the recent plethora of relevant theoretical literature from leading colleagues, I am pursuing my own experiential emphases. My formula has many parallel forms: negotiation, empathy and interpretation; or just dependency, merging and autonomy; or work, love and play.

I now choose the theme of *pace* with its implicit idea of self pacing as a possible platform and pathway underneath and through all of the mentioned objectives and fulfillments in psychotherapy. I am indebted to Theodor Reik (1937, 1945) for alerting us to that keynote which contains the concomitant foci on self experiencing and interweaving in the external world or its mental representations. Such coexistence keeps one's consciousness oscillating between the intrapsychic and the adaptive processes while signalling our attention to another, perhaps both primary and ultimate, agency in being a person. I speculate here on the workings of that originating power of attorney because it seems to recognize the authority of both inner tensions and outer pressures as well as to be able to call on energies, directions and forms which derive from beyond, below and above, identifiable resources and opportunities. *Pace* suggests a private rhythm and so has a biological tenor as well as a planning motif; it may suggest a meeting ground, a play space for the functions of body and the mental forces. This agency tries to know everything, inside and out, but is never fully knowable, never completely expressible, never finished, whenever we attend one another, even in the deepest encounter. The crucial quality is a private pacing, allowing for both a change of pace and a pacing of those changes.

The first hint I know of its existence is in the phenomena of "the quiet alert state" in the infant (Wolff, 1959). That apparent, aware peace (*pace*, in Latin) signifies the person beyond instinct and beyond relationship. It is frequently energized and disturbed by drive, effort or engagement, whether joyous or traumatic. Curiously, there are various schizoid, even autistic, conditions which yield moments hinting at its persisting presence in the midst of the most pathological conditions. I suggest that the primary person is never dead, never totally absent. The basic challenge to the psychotherapist is to allow, invite, its renewal of active functioning for its own "sake." The American Heritage Dictionary defines *sake:* purpose, motive, end; advantage, good; personal benefit or interest, welfare; contention, lawsuit, guilt. What else can a person basically want or do, ever? In the beginning of being is the seed and model of the fullest and final becoming. The new sensitivities from recent infant observations (especially in Chapter IV) bring us closer to those mysteries. Are we ready to bear a renewal of concern with "man's soul" (Bettelheim, 1984)?

Thus do I ground the ethic of my professional activity, and more. I see the new patient as feeling he has lost touch with his pace of personhood and hoping to find it again. The infinite varieties of presented sufferings and hidden self deceptions are the cloudy, confused and even clamoring calls for help, the individually biased creations of corrupted and crippled efforts to reclaim the source, the aim and the object which he promised himself when born in moments of "primary love." I am indebted to Michael Balint for evoking this springboard in his writings from 1932 to the end. Above this general ground level hypothesis, the patient presents us with his particular melange of explanatory messages, which are traditionally differentiated into diagnostic perspectives that prompt particular procedures or "techniques." To respect the individualized patterns of narratives with etiological formulations, those diagnostic labels, which are justified as a shorthand among experienced experts, run the serious risk of reinforcing our role playing. The patient's presenting a passive position leaves him vulnerable to our authority and he is likely to suspend, to bury more deeply, his own measuring and defining of his primary objectives. How can we reestablish his active functioning as the agent, the person in charge of himself in the world? A later essay here resumes the theme of practicing psychotherapy without the crippling crutches of diagnostic classifications.

For now, I remain with the broader principles of an ethic emphasizing self responsibility. That hoary, ancient chestnut from Socratic philosophy, *know thyself*, needs fresh roasting and toasting as we redefine the self to be known. I submit that we may, for present sake or advantage, move further from pronouncing the objects of human desire and develop more ways to attend, invite, evoke the self awareness of currents and layers of feeling tones. Of course affect is not the whole story but I would trust to the patient's wish to make his own narrative meanings as far and as full as he feels willing. We may later join in, if invited, to shape, revise and confirm the emerging explanations he seeks; we can play together in this way and perhaps foster hints and elements of reflecting and speculating as models he may internalize selectively for his own self regulating exercise, at his own pace and for his own sake, together or separately. His efforts to know himself are far more reliable and usable than are ours. We do our most valuable work, in my view, eliciting his consciousness of the texture of feeling notes surrounding his words and behaviors while with us.

By presenting himself voluntarily he invites our sensing the presence of his affect, even as he may confuse and conceal some of it. We are being asked, I think, to note his helpless distorting, his disordering and his compromising his messages, and to help him come through, as did the first caretaker to some degree, or he would not have survived to complain. If we respect that surface level of communicating, his feeling tones, he may, feeling safer about our regard for his elusive personhood, his being in charge, allow a fuller expression of additional elements and layers of his private experience. He needs confirmations from the sensitive empathic attending with which we accompany him further in his untangling his path to greater self knowledge. He wants to be in charge even of occasions and ways of not being in charge, as when he lends his personhood to the therapist. These are my ethical assumptions.

Many of us are trying to develop a theory of affects. The working hypothesis I am exploring and trying to implement here is that the patient comes basically for assistance in identifying, expressing, reflecting on and modifying his feelings; this is his prime objective in psychotherapy. Our psychoanalytic heritage, with its discoveries about transference processes for affects and affect-laden images and representations, can be advanced by a more consistent patience in that function of observing for feeling tones from the surface down to fragments of feeling. Usually the cues are contained in the patient's narratives, reflections and affective decisions. So we guess about the affect, the qualities of openness and aliveness, the range of expressiveness, and the connectedness between feeling tone and the verbalized messages accompanying. We hold our hunches ready for the nod, the look, the word, the pause which hints at a possible invitation to offer our impression, of course, tentatively. A gentle touch in our style of stating our observations will keep the patient's space freer and more fluid for his activeness to his ends, so that he directs the flow of his efforts to recognize his affects and manage the images and energies constituting his complaints and desires.

I remember how Darwin concluded his researches on *The Expression of Emotions* (1872) with three principles of psychotherapeutic value, for regaining "mental elasticity." He approaches several aspects of current dynamic theories and methods:

> The movements of expression give vividness and energy to our spoken words. They reveal the thoughts and intentions of others more truly than do words, which may be falsi-

fied. . . . The free expression by outward signs of an emotion intensifies it. On the other hand, the repression, as far as this is possible, of all outward signs softens our emotions. He who gives way to violent gestures will increase his rage; he who does not control the signs of fear will experience fear in a greater degree; and he who remains passive when overwhelmed with grief loses his best chance of recovering elasticity of mind. (p. 365)

For the therapeutic dialogue, the refining of the data of feelings constitutes the major medium of exchange and also becomes the mode for effective change. Darwin deserves the title, "grandfather of modern psychotherapy" (Shor, 1963 and 1963a).

Darwin expected that neurology and physiology would eventually objectify our understanding of "the source or origin of the various expressions" of emotions (1872, p. 366). Freud suspended that view and came to recognize a far greater private variability in his review and redefinition of the dynamics of psychic trauma, in 1926:

Clearly, it [the essence and meaning of a danger situation] consists in the subject's estimation of his own strength compared to the magnitude of the danger and in his admission of the helplessness in the face of it. . . . In doing this he will be guided by the actual experiences he has had (whether he is wrong in his estimation or not is immaterial for the outcome). (SE Vol. XX, p. 166).

For the analytic therapist, slow, careful empathy about feelings must be the limits to his interventions until the patient invites his ally to suggest tentative hypotheses. Treating transferences with respect for possible plausibilities (Gill, 1982) sustains the working alliance while giving the patient's agenthood priority. Spitz's warning of the dangers in infant observation, that "meaning is arbitrarily imposed by us" (1984, p. 315) has at least equal significance for the work of the analyst. We may be asked to make guesses about the *quality* of the affect but we surely must be patient and remain silent about the inner intensities, the *quantitative* aspects of the affects. Early, Freud concluded that

> It is true we are unable to measure this amount of libido which seems to us indispensible for a pathogenic effect; we can only postulate it after the resulting illness has started. (1912, SE Vol. XII, p. 236)

More broadly, he alerted us " . . . from a knowledge of the premises we could not have foretold the nature of the result. . . . What we know about them is only their quality and not their relative strength. . . . To predict it . . . is impossible" (1920, SE Vol. XVIII, pp. 167-8). Ernest Jones quotes Freud, writing to Marie Bonaparte: I hover, so to speak, in the air; mental events seem to be immeasurable and probably always will be so (Biography of Freud, V. II, p. 419)

Perhaps not "always." In 1986, C. B. Pert, chief of brain bio-chemistry, Clinical Neuroscience Branch, National Institute of Mental Health, wrote:

> One last speculation, an outrageous one perhaps, but on the theme I was asked to consider for this symposium on "Survival and Consciousness." Can the mind survive the death of the physical brain? Perhaps here we have to recall how mathematics suggests that physical entities can suddenly collapse or infinitely expand. I think it is important to realize that information is stored in the brain, and it is conceivable to me that this information could transform itself into some other realm. . . . Where does the information go after the destruction of the molecules (the mass) that compose it? Matter can neither be created nor destroyed, and perhaps a biological information flow cannot just disappear at death and be transformed into another realm. Who can rationally say "impossible"? The mathematics of consciousness have not ever been approached. The nature of the hypothetical "other realm" is currently in the religious or mystical dimension where Western science is clearly forbidden to tread" (p. 16).

When Freud pronounced that "the conscious ego . . . is first and foremost a body-ego" (S.E. XIX, p. 27) he leaves space and time for a prior agency, not simply the unorganized ID or instinctual components. His acceptance of limitations to speculation, to be open to the full play of patients' hypotheses decades ago, need not discourage our present respect for subjectivities beyond our own experience or conviction. Having gained from previous advances, including Freud's, we may be ready to afford a humbler ethic toward others, a more modest approach to patients than has been institutionalized as classical analytic technique.

VIII

The Case of Dream
Interpretation (Kris)

Freud's *Interpretation of Dreams* is viewed as the epitome of
hermeneutics, calling on subtle and elaborate explications for
the deepest secrets of the person. I propose to approach the
reporting of dreams as a special form of playing, not as coded
messages. While he lived, there was little publication about
the interpreting of dreams. Then, friends and opponents of
psychoanalysis began to take to the precious function of eluci-
dation and denucleation of secret meanings in the dream content, all implying agreement with Freud's early heralding of
this "royal road to the unconscious." Perhaps too much awe has
been given those mysterious night messages and we remain in
wondrous regard, as is often given difficult poetry. Our clinical
approach here may be less magical, but perhaps more therapeutic in character.

I remember how, in the midst of delicate responsibilities
for military intelligence in the early 1940s, Ernst Kris, that
bright star in Freud's last "circle" of colleagues, asked me to
assist in his large project on "Freud's Theory of the Dream in
American Textbooks" (Kris, Herma and Shor, 1943). We spent
dozens of hours each month for nearly a year, researching the

data and refining our analyses of four decades of professional responsiveness to Freud's original accomplishment. We found that only slowly was any positive regard for Freud's book given in academic circles. Most explicit comments were critical, yet the interest continues to mount.

Dream interpretation has been widely viewed as the heart of the mythology of psychoanalysis. The worshipful and magical attitudes to psychoanalytic theory have even focused on the first dream presented in depth psychotherapy as the key to the basic personality of the patient; it was declared as the guide to the central task for the therapist. A doctoral study of this hypothesis (Repko, 1975) focused on *Spontaneous and Forced Dreams in the Therapeutic Process* and allowed a critical examination of the method and ethics of obtaining dream data. Before we consider the specific issues of that research and their implications for my general thesis here, I will review some background of this arena in the history of psychoanalysis, as a contrast to my approach. I do not suggest any special interest or value in dreams when meeting with a patient. One may guess that the actual practices with regards to dream material are very variable and rarely discussed formally, so the myths are protected from full examination.

One early, and persisting, stereotype for dream analysis favors a kind of ritual for exhaustive free associations to every element in the text reported. Clearly Freud's 1900 edition fostered such rites as he pursued his self analysis and his fresh hypotheses about infantile wishes in psychic structure and functioning. The metapsychological discoveries he constructed have been put to work, by him and by most psychoanalysts, until the recent rebellions against drives, instincts and metapsychology in general, including primary processes. Whatever will be the judgements of our next generations, the preoccupation with ferreting out fine hidden details has been revived this last decade or two, even to recast Freud's private personality and the character of his relationships to colleagues. So that first formal model of dream study continues to serve archaic purposes even if Freud moved on to more balancing attitudes and procedures. Hobson (1988) makes a biological attack on pre-emptive uses of dream theory, but he goes too far; he neglects body functions as symbols of higher meanings for the whole self.

Freud did proceed to advise us against treating dream data as special (SE. XII, pp. 91–96; XIX, pp. 102–121; et. al.) asking us rather to attend above all and consistently to the transference cues at hand, within and surrounding all reports. Kaplan (1989) generally agrees. In 1925, Freud even bemoans " . . . when I think of all the mischief some analysts have done with the interpretation of dreams I might lose heart . . . " (SE, XX, p. 193). As late as 1931, he admits that his first explorations of this original procedure did serve him well personally, that it all was "very special to me," but he lived to regret having given out such internal data.

Since his death several even loyal followers have presumed to ignore his preference for privacy. Others have also reinvestigated his published dream fragments and used private correspondence to produce powerful attacks on his character, commiting unprincipled displays of personal heresy. I choose not to name the authors of these rude invasions, to be consistent with my ethical principles. I choose to protect my "Freud" and select those public statements which fit my perspective.

For a 1981 conference on "The Dream After 80 Years" at UCLA, the title for my workshop was a note of warning, "Some Dangers in Analyzing Dreams." It must be admitted, and considered, that very few of the attendees chose to discuss so discouraging an attitude; perhaps we need to hold sacred some sources for our forays into the subjectivities of human experiencing. In any case, this case especially, I remind you of Freud's disavowals of the royal road to favor the more sensitive and modest following of transference styles; not talmudic disputations on covert dream contents but respectful attendence to the complexities blocking private puzzles.

In 1933, in his *New Introductory Lectures*, Freud complains of the lack of interest in dreams in the psychoanalytic literature. Kris, in a 1954 conference notes Freud's worry and complains about the absence of new developments for dream theory. Perhaps that public silence signified a repressive respect for what had been declared to be a great personal value to the father. Fifteen years after Freud's death, Robert Waelder reported a renewal of attention, at the Symposium on Dream Interpretation by the American Psychoanalytic Association (1954). His book (1954) is titled *The Revival of Interest in Psychoanalysis and Dream Analysis.* That year Erikson also published his view of the problem:

> The art and ritual of exhaustive dream analysis has all but vanished and the advancement of the technique of psychoanalysis is a major reason for it. There is now a new therapeutic zeal which is based on our new understandings of transference and resistance and our ability to observe it in detail.

This keynote does move us toward my concerns with subjectivity and ethical relating, rather than keep us in bondage to possible hidden meanings in a mysterious text. Erikson has greatly enriched our appreciation of the spiral dialectic of phases of human motivation, accommodations, compromises and creative surges; his contributions are rooted in the developmental perspective begun in Freud's Chapter VII of *The Interpretation of Dreams.* Beyond Freud, he has equipped us for a fuller empathy with the qualities of experiencing the common struggles in most stages of growth and maturation. To add the notice about subjective transference tendencies does take us near a quite radical position about interpreting dreams; Erikson does assert, in that article, that even periodic emphasis on dreams is wasteful and may be deleterious to psychotherapy. He suggests that to choose to use dream data is an expression of a scarcity feeling, not of a choice from abundance in the work with patients. I add now, it may be a desperate gesture, perhaps complicating the analysis iatrogenically.

This extreme position needs some balancing here. I would agree, somewhat, with Erikson's remarks in 1954, that in training candidates intensive seminars with examples of exhaustive dream interpretations may serve to illustrate the experience of discovering cues to new concepts, as Freud did. This training experience may stimulate a research attitude for our field but I think it unfair to exploit patients by insisting on that archaic, sterotypic practice. It complicates the patient's transference and makes for iatrogenic burdens to his therapeutic efforts and interests.

Here, I do appreciate Erikson's further suggestion that consistent dream interpretation may be most useful in self analysis. Freud used it so but unfortunately gave out some of his personal data, which he came to regret. Self analysis is inherently the source, the aim and the object of psychoanalytic therapy, in my view; this private process can repair the damages and fill in the gaps which any professional therapy experience will precipitate to some degree. Even if the "countertransference" complications in self analysis compound the variables, the one agent, the person constitutionally has the right and is in the best space for making the most of the infinite complexities; he knows and cares more closely for more of the hidden forces at play. We, outside that private place and process, may be given glimpses, always screened by the context of the telling.

Here is the core for my worries about the use of dream interpretation in psychotherapy: the risk of neglecting the specific transferential context for the reporting. The opportunity to test my emphasis on such ethical concerns came when I was asked to supervise a doctoral candidate's dissertation at a local university in 1974–75. Glen Repko had formulated the research question, perhaps influenced by talks I had given. He reviewed the variety of practices, formulated or implied, in professional publications, for obtaining that precious dream data in ways other than by a mechanistic instruction at the start of psychotherapy to "bring your dreams in." Such instructional procedure is rarely reported but left implicit. We'll never know the whole story about another's practices.

However the stereotype is in our culture and some patients assume, expect and comply with it, whether or not specifically instructed. However, earnest submission need not be welcomed or accepted as a sudden gift; the preliminary negotiations I've described in earlier chapters set a tone which allows us to verbalize the apparent choice and to openly agree to proceed with the patient's preference. I want him to know that he has initiated the format and that I am not recommending or discouraging, but ready to "Let's try and see how it goes." But let me suspend my repetitious preaching and return to Repko's study for his findings.

He noted various styles of suggesting the special value of reporting dreams; from "It could help me in our work" to "It sometimes can be valuable for us." More usually, nothing specific is said in advance but when it first occurs, from whatever subtle pressures, from within or without, the therapist may spring to attention and become specially active and inquiring in the spirit of searching for the secrets or of solving a major puzzle. Patience seems suspended as several role playing performances by the analyst are reinforced in the patient's mind. The subject's submission brings to mind Balint's critique of the classical "ocnophilic (clinging dependency) bias" (1959) in analytic psychotherapy. Reading Balint's analysis of that iatrogenic transference was a major experience influencing my move towards the British Independents, and to London for several years.

Back to Repko; he was working in a clinic where low cost psychotherapy was available and he had frequent opportunities to work with self supporting clients. He set up three modes of initiating the therapies:

1. A nearly classical "Do bring in your dreams as soon as you can."
2. "Whenever you remember any dream, do include your memory of it as you free associate."
3. No reference to possible dream data and no special interest to be manifested if one is mentioned.

In the course of about two years, he had gathered the first dream for each of eight patients in each of the three modes. These dreams were described in their references to persons and activities, the details given, the attitudes and feelings alluded to—in all, a kind of surface context analysis of the reports. Since there are obvious selective processes in such exploratory studies of depth clinical experiencing, we do not apologize for the limited analysis but rather look for hints of possible tendencies suggestive of the effects of the three approaches.

The results, in brief, are supportive of our anticipation that the more self-regulating style, mode three, yielded far fuller dreams, richer in affective detail and references to past, to current and to transference events; also, more free associations were spontaneously given. These patients seemed to claim a freer playground for self expression and self exploring for inside and external linking of elements of feeling, complaints and desires. The more forced dream material, modes one and two, was generally shorter, with specific, crisp references to surface, everyday events; no hints of the therapist's presence, little about the past or any puzzling affects.

Am I overworking this small sample of artificial data? My hand is on the table open to reach and touch lightly the hints I am seeking. I am fitting the few pieces yielded by this research into the soft contours of the basic approach I am favoring. I am happy to report that the university approved the dissertation and granted the doctorate degree. A mixed result, perhaps? Soft data and mushy conclusions?

In 1953, Ernst Kris wrote that the growing acceptance of psychoanalytic ideas in the academic world would water down the richness of its meanings and theories. By then, I was not unhappy about a decrease of demands for hard precision in a field in which the data are largely subjective. I had been on the faculty of four universities, and there would be several more to this date, but my part-time indulgences in that rationalistic academic environment was a symptom of my wish to be nourished by both emphases, the clinical and the academic, and perhaps a wish to contribute to both, to bridge the gap with more flying buttresses. In Freud's very subtle and delightful *The Question of Lay Analysis*, he suggests that formal degrees, there, the medical degree, and I now add the doctorate in general, perhaps any social crutch of authority status, "are all sometimes curable obstacles to becoming a good psychoanalyst" (Shor, 1961). Well, I'm still at work, trying.

I'm not asking that we give up dream material but rather to respect the larger context of a complaining person wanting to use our assistance to regain his own authority for regulating his living processes. I will try to look to the problem of the inner "resistances" of the patient which obstruct his own aims, in a next chapter. Here I want to alert us to practices which create obstacles, iatrogenic complications to his efforts. So I remind us of the still to be fathomed reaches for transference analyses—and the preparatory phases, negotiations and empathies, which precede most effective analyses of transferences and useful constructions of narratives. Dream reports may or may not be given. When they are, the person may ask our hunches about some of the content; if invited, within an established, easy therapeutic alliance, we can respond with tentative hypotheses. If the relationship is not easy, we stay close to his troubled style of regarding us. This now very obvious principle points to the private responsibilities of the therapist to ask himself whether he may be imposing his own investment in role playing. No colleague, no outsider, can usefully decide for him, even if the professional returns to analysis. Ultimately it is a possibility best pursued in self analysis.

In dream seminars, I raise these questions though I do not wait for complete answers; only patients deserve my fullest professional patience. I ask:

- How is the dream data initiated or invited?
- What rituals are allowed to form and are they negotiated openly for their implied promises, images and feelings in process?
- When should dream content not be interpreted?
- Is the affect surrounding the act of reporting dreams noted and given preliminary attention?
- What characterological temptations are likely and discoverable for the giving and using dreams as sources of special insights?

For us here, I want to raise some further issues about the peculiarly difficult nature of dream reports. If we postulate an originally authentic quality to the actual experiencing of dreaming, we must recognize that many variables interfere with our knowing the original truth of that private experience. At the reporting in session, the account is a very selective memory, not necessarily more "accurate" than a story about a past incident, or a loaded current relationship event. No outside person can correct the errors or distortions in the given description. The affect told or evident in the telling may not really refer to the first edition; it is not a clearly ego-syntonic occasion of remembering. So we cannot reasonably claim to be interpreting *the dream,* only the telling.

For all the possible varieties of unconscious motivations to modify the original experience of dreaming in reporting it, we may succeed in identifying certain leading aspects currently pressing in the transference. But we would likely agree that other evidences, not dream-like, should be considered before we link any interpretation primarily to the dream offered to us. I do feel it is a serious error, an iatrogenic distortion, to foster the attitude that the dream is a special magical source of insight. Such bias removes the dialogue from the flexibilities of open playfulness and joint refining of inner currents of feeling, in pain or desire. The distance to the private dream is so elusive that we may have left the "playground" and not see any road markers for finding our way back at the end of the session. The patient may leave as in a trance, fascinated by the imaginative suggestions of the therapist demonstrating his skill in unlocking a rebus. The grounds are too soft and cloudlike, so a light, casual attitude about dream material may be protective, and leave room for the more immediate and direct experiencing of affect in the actual presence of the two persons at work together. REM dream studies hardly allow for such considerations.

We can catch ourselves moved to be clever or to be helpful at once to the puzzled patient telling us a perplexing night experience. I think a most useful and also honest response to a challenging report is to be reflective and alertly patient. The message is so multidimensional with a myriad of moments for reshaping the story, which is frequently revised and "corrected" as we go on. The patient can more easily recognize those specially elusive qualities in his accounts. His uneasiness about such unreliability deserves that respectful attending which can lead to freer expression as part of his struggle to help himself get better.

When Kris directed that 1941–43 study of dream theories, he formulated a concise summary of Freud's hypotheses to guide our sorting of colleagues' comprehension; Kris' outline is appended to the published report of our work (Kris, Herma and Shor, 1943). That framework is open to new findings and principles. I feel that much of my approach is integratable with that classical perspective; perhaps not all. The focal function of transference analysis, which Freud discovered substantially in formulating *The Interpretation of Dreams*, does keep psychoanalysis open to the refinements of even my flagrantly "ethical" emphasis. The ongoing expansion of ego psychology has finally moved us through the contentions between object relations theory and self psychology; Freud had anticipated this problem in 1921, advising that "in the individual mental life someone else is invariably involved" (SE XVIII, p. 69). Ernst Kris in his 1940–50 seminars at the Graduate Faculty of the New School for Social Research anchored his thinking on the idea of the ego as the "Home Defense Department" (much as I have come to define a primary function of the Person). He put to use the defensive focus of our joint work for American and British Intelligence during the war years. His charming playful attitudes were yet open to his genuine regard towards and adoption of contributions from colleagues as well as from assistants and students, as I was then. His style of expression was decades ahead of the formulations being shaped by the orthodoxy which welcomed his participation. Working with him daily in this project on Freud's dream theory, 1941–42, promoted some essentials of my present perspective. I do thank him.

From Kris' perspective on Freud's theory of the dream, I gained a broad sense of the dialectic of progress in social and individual development. Long before Freud, dreams were experienced as cues from above, divine messages. When our culture advanced in constructive narcissism and diminished the image of His omnipotence, dreams were seen as chance expressions of lesser processes. Then Freud added, crucially, the important roles of forces from within the socially liberated, newly independent person, from the dark conflictual and repressed realms.

For the past several centuries, we have been meeting those dangerous dimensions with our cultural eras of Humanism, Renaissance, Protestant Enlightenment, Rationalism, Romanticism, Science and Technology, Democratic Liberalism and now the Psychological Age with its psychoanalytic contributions (Shor, 1948).

Current concerns with interrelating and with intersubjectivity have directed us to the primary and prior processes of developmental and therapeutic exchanges, with the new sensitivities to "transference" and "counter-transference." These new awarenesses turn our attention first to the selective processes of communication in telling dreams as well. We no longer can maintain the worship of dream content, manifest or latent, as is usually implied in the hermeneutic attitudes which persist. We remember that Freud too gave up that image of dreams as the Royal Road to the Unconscious. It's a rocky road requiring a very careful attention to the interplay of attitudes between the two passengers on the therapeutic journey.

IX

Confronting Resistance Analysis

When one was ready to give up a Royal Road into the Unconscious, the therapeutic challenge became an emphasis on a less magical and more difficult path, that of resistance analysis. Even Freud sometimes equated resistance analysis with all or most of transference analysis. He has supported that equation with quasi-biological hypotheses about the repetition compulsion and thanatos while colleagues have added clinical cues about resistance from basic masochism (e.g. Reik, 1949); even "primary masochism" (Bergler, 1949).

Deliberate concern with clinical "resistence" haunts psychoanalytic literature since the very beginning and continues to this date. In his *Studies on Hysteria* (1895, SE II) Freud's chapter on "The Psychotherapy of Hysteria" is permeated with this practical problem and his evocative hypotheses for developing new methods beyond hypnosis and new theories beyond catharsis. We all know the richness of his productive speculations for all of later psychoanalysis. There are roots and clear cues to Ego psychology, and even specific intuitions about the central role of "the self feeling of the patient" (p. 92) to anchor improvements in psychotherapy. His intrapsychic framework would only slowly open up to the interrelational processes which have recently gained equal attention and vitalize both dimensions into the spiral dialectic which pervades the thinking of this decade.

A 1987 volume on *Techniques of Working with Resistance* (Milman and Goldman) contains the contribution of more than a dozen of today's leading thinkers, classical and innovative; the editors find little agreement and "a lack of central coherent, and organized models . . . as a frame of reference for understanding resistances" (p. 23), and they "do not attempt" to propose any promising directions for further progress.

I will suggest that a basic principle in the patient-therapist interplay is being ignored even though the clue was evident in Freud's first case study, his work with Emmy von N., in 1888 (SE II, pp. 48–105). In fact, I see in this remarkably honest and modest report the outline of the essential phases of the humanist approach to psychoanalytic therapy which is proposed here, decades after I first read his *Studies on Hysteria*.

Emmy von N. is described as "admirable. . . . her intelligence and energy . . . were no less than a man's . . . her high degree of education and love of truth . . . her benevolent care for the welfare of all her dependents, her humility of mind and the refinement of her manners revealed her qualities as a true lady as well" (pp. 103–104). Yet she expressed much resistance to Freud's instructions and manipulations of her body, even exclaiming at times, "Keep still!—Don't say anything!—Don't touch me!" (p. 49). Physician Freud responded with a flexible respect for brief periods before resuming his tentative exercise of his array of direct questions, prohibitions and somatic procedures, including hypnosis. In the second week of more than daily visits, the following sequence of events occurred:

> "I requested her to remember by tomorrow. She then said in a definitely grumbling tone that I was not to keep on asking her where this and that came from, but to let her tell me what she had to say. I fell in with this, and she went on without preface. . . . This had been the origin of her unsociability and her hatred of all strangers. After I had spoken some calming words about what she had told me, she said she felt easier. [Next morning] she was in a good mood (and) cheerful . . . She asked me my opinion about all sorts of things

that seemed to her important, and became quite unreasonably agitated, for instance, when I had to look for the towels needed in massage, and so on." (p. 63)

Note how these proceedings begin with active *negotiations*, initiated by the patient, about her rights and expertise about the subjective data which Freud was pursuing. She also demanded, against the tradition of medical practice, that she set the pace and direction of the process, that she be responsible for judging what feels important to her. Freud fortunately "fell in with this." When she paused he offered some *empathy*. Her mood changed and she then cheerfully invited him to give his understandings of further matters of significance to her, his tentative *interpretations*. When Freud prepares to resume the manipulative role, the massaging, the patient becomes agitated. Freud did not recognize the change of pace; nor did he identify the dialogue processes as such though he will in time intuit some of their humanistic assumptions.

In contrast to his response to Emmy, Freud's handling of Elizabeth von R. four years later, reported in the same volume (SE II, pp. 135–181), remains permeated with resistance until the patient, a girl of 24, gives up and submits. Freud apparently continued his "insistance," with much criticizing, threatening, confronting and promising "cure." The girl's family reinforced this authoritarian pressure. She was not a voluntary patient. Freud describes her as "a harsh character," "cheeky," "cocksure," "greatly discontented with being a girl," and "full of ambitious plans for her own development." He reports that "she resented her family's plans for her marrying" (all, p. 154). Freud sums up: "I regarded her as cured . . . she has married someone" (pp. 159–160). Resistance analysis is given birth in this case, and is given more overt emphasis, more than is given to the humanist and dialogue qualities till very recently.

The two Freuds, physician-scientist and psychotherapist-humanist, oscillate through his sixty years of life-work. Both positions are refined and deepened as advances in the one stimulate and equip the other. All the schools of psychoanalysis and the surrounding groups of counsellors, healers and psychotherapists represent variable ratios of objective expertise and subjective facilitation of self repair. Their controversies are forms of cultural dialogue despite the sometimes rude tenor of their exclusive attitudes. When Freud was challenged by legal authorities to define his viewpoint, he moved to his firmest exposition of Western liberalism for self determination in psychotherapy:

> It is left to the patient in all essentials to determine the course of the analysis and the arrangement of the material; any systematic handling of particular symptoms or complexes thus becomes impossible (SE XX, p. 41).

Here he rules out resistance analysis despite the heritage of professional authority which preceded and followed. Before tracing some of the dialectic shifts, I suggest that the increasing attention to empathy with the suffering and struggling self, and to the subjectivities in both patient and therapist, is evoking rich data for a psychological science beyond the fathomless depths of clinical psychotherapy. And yet, we are witnessing a proliferation of manipulative bio-chemical methods in psychiatry. Together these opposing trends are provoking neuroscience to adventurous hypotheses. I've referred to the daring speculations by the chief of brain biochemistry of the National Institute of Mental Health about "the mathematics of consciousness" into "the religious or mystical dimension" (Pert, p. 16). Playfulness is as essential for evolving the human experience including the changing certainties of scientific knowledge.

My search for next explorations in psychoanalytic therapy took me to arenas which my current colleagues avoided and resisted. I will report the viscissitudes in this chapter. The surface issues were the tolerances for fresh or loosely speculative approaches to patients in treatment; the hidden dilemmas were, and are, the challenges of the mind-body interplay as we recurrently redefine them.

The year after Freud declared his absolute defense of self-determination by the patient, he formulated his five types of resistance confronting the benign efforts of the psychoanalyst (SE XX, p. 160): *Id* repetition compulsion, *Ego* repression, transference and secondary gains, *Superego* guilt and need for punishment. The explanations and remedies for these resistances are less optimistic than his sometimes hopeful trusting to the wish for self-repair to overcome the self-deceptions. He calls on biological principles and presumptive estimates of human potentialities: Thanatos, masochism, the stickiness of unconscious conflicts and compromises and the negative therapeutic effects.

Later, he opens the field to a more modest definition of the therapist's functioning as subtle facilitator of the person's self measuring and self regulating (SE XXIII, p. 250), as with Emmy von N. From the many recent professional concerns with newly recognized qualities of interaction between therapist and patient, and from personal predilections, both alluded to in these essays, I am emphasizing the more optimistic task of favoring the patient's positive aims for himself and respecting his rights and responsibilities to feel in charge of his therapy. Over the years, Freud's writings do oscillate around such trusting attitudes, and I am reporting some of my vascillations and slips. But I see a dialectic spiral or double helix as inherent in development, with its moves for "scientific" safety and for "humanistic" freedom. I now stress the trend for richer "play."

My basic principle is to view the patient's symptoms and complaints all as containing the primary wish to repair oneself and one's relationships, not a tragic or cynical view of primary self obstructiveness and self destructiveness. The clinical obstacles to more benign intentions are to be seen as deep distrusts, earned and fantasied, about self and about the other, including the therapist. The task in practice is to first meet the doubts and distrusts with sensitive negotiations and then with flexible empathies which are to precede any interpretations, including transference and resistance analysis.

I have suggested that the roots for my approach are present in selected parts of Freud's writings and then in those of Kris, Reik and especially Balint, as representative of the

113

British tradition of Independents (Kohon, 1987). There are also partial cues to this direction in many more recent American writings (K. Menninger, L. Stone, H. Loewald, E. Schwaber, R. Schafer, W. Bion, M. Hack, R. Spitz, E. Erikson, L. Havens, A. Modell, S. Blatt, A. Lazare, H. Kohut, D. Stern, even Arlow and Brenner, and most especially, M. Gill and E. Caruth (see References), and others). I cannot do justice to these favorable developments in this context but clearly the move away from the classical focus on resistance analysis seems to be a gathering trend.

To broaden this trend, I will illustrate the process of liberating myself from the orthodox principle of emphasis on resistance analysis through my relationships to the ideas of my important teachers. This personal account may show some stages in identifying the larger ethical and practice issues which became clearer to me as I privately confronted my colleagues' resistances to my further explorations in the field.

My narrative of the journey from Kris to and through Reik is a somewhat turgid tale with implicit bits of ideological antagonism and pieces of painful disappointment about institutional rigidities. Each human being measures and defines the conditions felt to be needed for a good-enough atmosphere for fulfilling exchanges with valued others; we are all experienced patients. The "likely presence of errors and illusions" in our measures (Shor, 1972, p. 264) will influence the pace by which we enjoy the relating and then look about to consider moving on. Conceptual firmness in any dialogues may create recalcitrant obstinances and stubborn opposition; these are the kernels of resistance, not essentially different from the blocks we experience and meet in psychotherapy as well.

Both Kris and Reik confronted me with their established positions as I moved about to make my own ventures in new areas of thinking and research. Each time, I was moved toward the sad ending of the important relationship with them. The personal loadings for me were substantial, of course, and my disappointments were deep. I do not know and will not speculate on the inner aspects of their responses. But I will try to tease out from my reactions, in memory, the ideas in those

114

phases of professional change which can illuminate my present perspective, especially about that much emphasized classical principle of "analysis of the resistances," with which I no longer agree nor practice.

I had met Kris in 1940 within weeks of his arrival from England, after his flight from Vienna. In London, he was part of that final circle surrounding Freud and also he had been doing research for the B.B.C. project on fascist propaganda. Then he moved to New York in mid-1940 to develop a Rockefeller Foundation research group on totalitarian communication. While preparing for that war work on Intelligence, he presented seminars on psychoanalytic theories and applications. That first fall I took his seminar on psychoanalysis and art; we quickly appreciated one another, I think, and he took me on as assistant for several courses and then in some of his other activities.

Thus, at age 21, I felt a close involvement which, in time, yielded me some basic understanding of psychoanalytic theories in a variety of clinical and applied aspects. The rewards, already mentioned earlier, included more than two years of daily association while participating in the Rockefeller research on communication, acceptance for training in the New York Psychoanalytic Institute and a guiding friendship which continued for more than a decade. It began to be complicated when I refused his advice to go through medical school. Lawrence Kubie had obtained for me an appointment as Therapist and Instructor at Yale Department of Psychiatry to begin at once. I decided not to spend years in medical training. Also I later refused to sign the belittling oath suddenly required by the American medical hierarchy against the spread of "lay analysis." When non-medical candidates were asked to restrict their roles to "research," I replied: "In psychoanalysis there has existed from the very start an inseperable bond between cure and research" (Freud, SE XX, p. 257). Therefore I was asked to leave the New York Institute in the midst of my analytic training. Kris said he thought he was the last Ph.D. that would be tolerated. He wanted me to play his game for my sake. My sake resisted and I moved on cautiously but with private determination to decide for myself. Kris' "guidance" and the stance of the analytic establishment were felt to be intrusions and constrictions, the core of my resistance.

The years with Kris were a reverberating dialogue about ideas, not technical instruction. Our intellectual exchanges were richly respectful of my development at my pace, but it was to be in his direction. What was missing for me was the other dimension of the Primary Illusion, my full autonomy for other directions as well. The dialectical spiral could not emerge into unfamiliar professional realms, such as seemed possible with Theodor Reik, who explicitly favored openness in his *Surprise and the Psychoanalyst* (1937) and *Listening with the Third Ear* (1945), the Americanized equivalent or translation.

Reik had appeared on the American scene toward the end of World War II, after a brief stay in England, also following his flight from Vienna. His works had begun to be translated from the German some years earlier and his, to me, most significant book, *Surprise and the Psychoanalyst*, was translated for British publication in 1937. His first American publication was *A Psychologist Looks at Love*, in 1944; which I had been asked to review for the American Psychological Association. We worked together to form a non-medical analytic institute until 1955. Then he opposed my interest in exploring the possible values of W. Reich's work. Perhaps that was beyond the limits of his tolerance for a competitor's ideas; his stubborn position faced me with a choice about submitting to or defying a friendly colleague's private rigidities. Reik's expertise in his very well regarded book, *Dogma and Compulsion*, did not prevent a wall of resistance from rising suddenly between us at a sad display of surprising unfriendliness in 1955. He voted against our Institute's tolerating my exploring for any valuable links between W. Reich's ideas and classical orthodoxy.

The strands of my accounts about these important teachers are overlapping in significance and affiliation as perhaps is usual in the texture of all experiencing in memory and reconstructions. We sort and shift already slivered and many times symbolized pieces of being in order to convert the flexible melange into a stream of becoming. "Resistance" is the stopping of any forward moving fluidity. The "Home Defense Department" (Kris) goes on full war alert, and when the therapist confronts this bulwark, in practice, the war is on and accelerating. If we are posing and believing that we are really the more powerful authority even for the patient's very private sores and parts, then we presume to act so; we see the patient as "resisting" our valuable insights. By hardening himself in further defense, the patient loses ground, and feels a loss of safe space for exploring and moving ahead by his own inner sensing and knowing, his own authority. He has lost his special ally, now turned against him. He feels pressured and threatened further, from outside. His greater desperation renders him even weaker and more vulnerable to being routed in the compounded battling. To save himself, for his own primary sake, he may concede an arm or a leg, or even a vital organ. The patient may yield until a later, stronger day, perhaps when he leaves us.

I assume, or hypothesize that the primary person, a Self or Ego, began before birth, before his body became public. We remember that Freud has pronounced that "the Ego is first and foremost a body ego" (1923). Was that dictum Freud's consolidation of a home base position so that he could advance his periscopes into some new territory, a next hill for observing and mapping the terrain ahead? He was making a plan and perspective for Ego Psychology in 1923. Since we cannot fight on all fronts at one time, deliberate suspensions and compromise consolidations can serve the sensible pacing. We select arenas of difficulty and of possible next discovery by temporarily conceding some openness or freedom for surprise. So did Kris withdraw as I moved to play some in Reik's less structured backyard.

The phenomena of pacing one's explorations and suspensions, were identified for Freud's life work by Edmund Bergler (1949a) who may be known best for his iconoclastic dancing about with ideas of primitive preoedipal dramas featuring "primary masochism" (1949b). Bergler proposed that Freud had suspended exploring the pre-oedipal phases as he developed his insights about oedipal dynamics. He then could focus full attention to the new task (Shor 1953). Freud had noted variables and vulnerabilities in pre-oedipal experiences as far back as his *Three Contributions to the Theory of Sex* (1905) where source, aim and object were identified as open to selective and contingent forces, and he had begun to see the infant's subtle processes of internalizing and identifying with the caretakers in several of his works. But then, says Bergler,

> . . . great discoveries are performed according to the principle of inner defense . . . Was it not the dichotomy of mothers (so clearly expressed in Goethe's *Fragment*) *which lent itself to the unconscious purpose of asserting the domination over the Oedipal mother to ward off the "schrecklechkeit" of the pre-Oedipal mother?* (Bergler, 1949; italics in text)

Here Bergler lends his perspective and pace to Freud but the more conservative New York Psychoanalytic Society kept Bergler in chains, as he put it to me in the several supervisor sessions I had with him. He was not invited to present his exploratory ideas on primary masochism to his colleagues, though both Henry Bunker, a former president of the Society, and the well respected training analyst, Ludwig Jekels, did appreciate the fresh winds arising, and joined Bergler in some writings (Jekels, 1953). Bergler complied with the constraints only in surface ways, I think. I saw him as very angry and "resisting" the authorities who imposed on him. I felt him assuming an authoritarian style in self defense, as he developed his independent pioneer formulations, which might yet return him a title as a first American Kleinian.

Both Bergler and M. Klein broke barriers with styles that were difficult, perhaps inevitably. Both battled official resistances and perhaps were responding with self balancing contortions. Again, style and pace may be the telling considerations for ideological fracas such as these, or for those much smaller editions I met from Kris, and later from Reik.

I did feel conflicts of loyalty as I tried to gain from the several sources. As I chose further analysis with Reik, leaving the stricter New York Society with their confining, assigned offerings and instructions for controlling my professional ambitions, Kris turned away and developed his own very valuable last lustrum of creative work. He performed major diplomatic work in formulating his progressive thesis, "Regression in the Service of the Ego"; no longer limited by the ever high-minded formula from Freud's pace of progress, "Where Id was, there shall Ego be." A third formula by Balint was later to startle me onto a new plane: "Progression for the sake of Regression." But for then I saw Kris' flexibility helpful to some in his orthodox group to be more open in the direction of benign regression, which is a cardinal principle for Michael Balint, but Kris did not open towards Reik's literary elaborations of the rich deep promises in wondrous vistas where he heralded "The Courage Not to Comprehend" (last chapter 1937). Some of us see in Reik sources for the later work of W. Bion, who worked on the margin between Klein's postulates and the preferences of the British tradition of Independents (Kohon, 1986).

Returning to our main theme here, we know how Freud had early recognized pre-oedipal problems and also expressed some of his early (1908) feminist perspective but he suspended these themes to foster the oedipal theme and develop an abstract metapsychology. He suffered ideological and sociological antagonisms as well as new forms of resistance in patients. Again, and perhaps always, the private pace and the public style conflict as one reaches for *both* free self expression and close dialogue with colleagues. Entrenched resistances only delay the movement, and confrontation compounds the stalemate; from these recognitions I began to tone down the boldness necessary to pursue resistance analysis in practice. Things became muddy.

Soon after Reik pronounced me a trained psychoanalyst, I made a pilgrimage to Vienna and found a possibly symbolic expression of Freud's pacing his interests, as Bergler had described. It was a statuette in a fountain in his back yard, where he faced this suggestive representation of a young and anxious girl. This undeveloped person obviously needed protection before she could flower. The male would first make safe space.

Some oedipal resolution must precede the exposure of pre-oedepal wishes. I photographed the statuette and en route home, to New York, I stopped off in London and told and showed my discovery to Ernst Jones, who was then writing the official biography of Freud. Responding to his interest I sent him a reprint of my tale about "A Wellspring of Psychoanalysis" (Shor, 1953). He reported my hypotheses (Vol. II, p. 381) and then added: "I could think of many rebuttals to this extraordinary idea, but I will leave the choice to my readers." Good enough, I felt. Jones had encouraged the British Society to know the stimulation of early Melanie Klein's rich and provocative theories and methods about the pre-oedipal; and he didn't totally dismiss my speculations.

I continue to value highly the more tolerant and flexible British attitudes toward human possibilities, including contentiousness, and I see that English tradition (Kohon, 1986) generally opposed to confrontative analyses of resistances as unfortunate and wasteful. I think confrontation derives from a more desperate, totalitarian tradition still lacking the safe space it needs to let up its hard lines of battling; such an authoritarian spirit denies its urgencies and externalizes its strains into taut impositions of rules on to vulnerable others. Perhaps to claim decisive cultural distinctions for such valuable attitudes is another forced imposition, a piece of sociological gossip.

The resisting patient, especially when feeling confronted, is demonstrating a healthy opposition to impositions. His person is being violated as the therapist picks on pieces of personality which are surface compromises by a self which feels lost or abused from its own history of misattunements and dissonant dialogues, its own accumulated traumas. When such feelings emerge in patients, I retreat empathically to his wish for safer grounds, for home base, and I speculate gently about lost or injured dreams and desires, the world of positive primary wishes. Employing the terms of his discontents, the specific painfulnesses in his complaints, I suggest the possible repairs which my set of hypotheses and assumptions for his essential personhood will select for this case at this time. I state my invited interventions as my guesses for a possible solution, not as established or precise truths and certainly not as finger-wagging admonitions or as confrontations; any such announced "insights" would be further insults to his own forward-moving intents, which I assume to be ultimate forces.

Without these softer, optimistic principles, I would be unwilling to bear the burden of depth, psychoanalytic psychotherapy. The challenge is fundamentally to my supply of easy patience. When I fail the patient in this dimension, I do apologize, express regrets, but also with appreciation for his resisting any aggressive or seductive gestures. I then wait to see whether he forgives me and reinvites our working alliance. I surely have lost some patients for reasons of style and pace, whether I tried to discuss these issues or not. Perhaps these essays are also a wider apology.

To resume the story of the dialectic spirals of subtle resistances in my professional, conceptual development, I turn back to a curious event of about 1943 when both clinical psychology and psychoanalysis were not yet of much significance in our popular culture or in the intellectual and academic worlds. Even a slightly experienced practitioner might be accorded, if teasingly, the role of an expert in new realms. A psychoanalyst had been appointed Chief Psychiatrist of the U.S. Army, W.C. Menninger, as the resistances of draftees, who produced neurotic defenses against military dangers, confounded the authorities who were showing a new tolerance for private complaining. This cultural advance towards psychoanalysis was a risky step for the American Home Front but we may have become ready for more patience for the tasks of investigation of and concern for the fresh, resistant soldiers. A few of us were given commissions to signify official responsibility for the unmanageable patients.

Decked in such kudos, I was asked by the Editor of the *Psychological Bulletin*, the official Review Journal of the American Psychological Association, a small society anticipating great expansions, to help him decide whether it would be "appropriate" to review two books by authors "who held themselves out to be psychologists." The two were: Theodor Reik's

The Psychologist Looks at Love, and Wilhelm Reich's *The Function of the Orgasm.* I found psychological value in both works and after writing to this effect, the Editor agreed only to the Reik book and asked whether I would do the review. I did so (1944). I told of Reik's boldly critical comments on aspects of Freud, the unsolved gaps between sex and love, and I added Reich's contrasting hypotheses for integrating the mind-body dilemmas in this problem.

I did not foresee that Kris, my then current teacher and friend, would finally distance himself from me nearly ten years later because of my participation in forming the non-medical psychoanalytic institute under Reik; nor could I have anticipated that Reik, in 1955, would put me aside because I wished to have Lowen, a late disciple of Reich, come address our Society, and neither discussed the issues with me and I did not confront them. I resisted neither of these dismissals, but moved away slowly, sadly, patiently, if I may say, to seek new companions for more rewarding dialogues. Fortunately, I had begun my close correspondence with Michael Balint, in London; but this follow-up tale later.

Memories skip back and forth through the spirals and funnels of time, moved by primary motivations renewed. We try to repair later trauma by recourse to earlier hopes and encouragements, through benign regressions. Reik had been pleased enough by my review; he immediately invited me to visit with him. He then gave me a copy of his *Surprise and the Psychoanalyst;* this vital and classical contribution to "the inner experience of the psychoanalyst" is still neglected, I think. His message for patience may yet be too bold for the orthodox establishment battle lines for safe space and formulating offensive technical weapons. The *Surprise* book is perhaps the most direct ancestor to these essays though I think I've found and gathered concepts and clinical experiences that were not available when Reik's book was written, over fifty years ago.

To return to the central theme here, the troubles with resistance analysis for both therapeutic and ethical values, I will recall another professional relationship, one where there was no cycle of submission, affiliation, dedication, excursion and then dismissal. This time with Moses Barinbaum, I had little sense of being adopted, instructed or constrained or graduated and yet I experienced the most authentic qualities of good analysis without the imposed crises of resistance analysis. I had asked him to be my supervisor for about a year. I claimed my pace and style and I appreciated his. Before, during and after, we were friends and shared social and professional gatherings with much comfort and ease between us. Moses Barinbaum was a quiet, soft person in spite of his also having to escape the Nazi holocaust. He had published very little, like Ludwig Jekels, that very valuable control analyst I had also selected for my sake, some two years earlier. Barinbaum had published a little, about psychosomatic symptoms, but it was his way of being and of commenting on clinical problems with respect for the patient which attracted me. Though a medical doctor as well as a member of the New York Psychoanalytic Society, he agreed to my request for some supervision of my analytic cases, in 1952–1953.

At our first session, he asked for no notes, no case history, no report of general progress or obstacles in the course of my past months of work with the patient. He asked simply how I *felt* about the most recent session. Given license to shape the session to the agenda I chose in asking for some supervision, I relaxed deeply and reflected freely on the texture of my experiencing the patient. He noted my hesitations, my shifts in focus or theme and any uneasinesses as I associated my way along internal private lines of concern or pleasure. His empathic alertings were like questions as to "What might that be about?" He didn't presume to take charge of my relationship to the patient, or to him. In that large middle space, he "let me tell what I felt might be important", as did Emmy von M. insist from Freud (1895). Barinbaum was my Freud in these central dimensions of the best ethical qualities in our work together.

In our next session (or was it the third?) I entered his nice, cozy, tasteful office and gave a passing glance to his couch. As I paused, Barinbaum asked, "Would you like to try proceeding from the couch?" "Yes," I accepted, and resumed reflecting about the previous session with the patient. Again, he intervened gently only to cue me to his guesses that some special or difficult affect of mine might be intruding into the free flow of my associations. These experiences, for about a year, made real for me personally the ideas about benign regression which I was just then reading about in Balint's first book, *Primary Love and Psychoanalytic Technique* (1952). I felt that theory and practice could be consonant, resonant and well attuned. I did return to Barinbaum for some further personal analysis soon after and felt renewed in both private and professional developing. My predilections for fuller theoretical formulations kept me looking for public statements of larger principles and theoretical considerations, more than the heartwarming and mind-freeing clinical style which Barinbaum offered. But we remained good friends until his death in the late 1950s. He sometimes would chide me with light, playful remarks about "those purple passages" in my publications; but I do think my pace and style has been changing some this last decade. To this day, I sometimes imagine conversations and friendly glances with gentle, patient, smiling Barinbaum.

Colleagues ask: How can you ignore the work of resistance analysis? Even most friendly colleagues express worry that I may be evading the cardinal task of depth psychotherapy! I tell them of my discomfort in doing the clever confrontations and subtle debunking which are considered to be necessary weapons for exposing self deceptions in the patient's economy. I try to resist such power politics and the exploitation of a patient's vulnerability. I remind myself that I cannot really know best, and that it would increase our battling if he senses any such presumption, though he rarely dares to say so. The stalemates that often consolidate at such points of discomfort may be relieved in time if the analyst eases up in his confrontations. The patient may then let up on his resistance. Whether in resignation or a fresh dose of decency, the less insistent therapist signals some patience and tolerance by carrying on quietly and allowing the strains of confrontation to subside. The patient may interpret the subsiding as his victory, or as the therapist's humble apology. Perhaps more often, as Ferenczi suggests in his "Confusion of Tongues" (1917) article, then the subject submits to the forced messages, internalizes, and spouts back the "correct" insights as his own. If he does not feel a manic unity with the leader, he may become depressed and mope along for a while for any "Ally," or any peace at any price.

In any case, the patient may gradually and cautiously renew his own efforts and hopes for another chance, or even a new beginning. He may open up some of the locked-off content which had festered inside the problematic "resistance" and make gains which are welcomed by both of them. Implicitly, he forgives the therapist's display of stubborn presumption, perhaps seeing those occasions as spats of bad manners beyond his control. I try to trust to the client's sense of ethics for himself rather than hold to an authortarian professional position. I remind myself that I am not experiencing the private cues and notes which only the patient possesses. He will lead the way into his own offensive inner resistances.

Permit me to narrate a final story for this theme of opposing a professional presumption of undoing patient's "resistances," which are always compounded of both internal cloggings and felt environmental impositions. This tale takes me back to the sixth grade of school. I remember the full name and the visual image of that classmate who challenged our teacher to stop complicating his relationship to his peers. He was the son of a teacher and had learned well the responsible manners of a good, bright pupil. Our teacher was having difficulties with obstreperous lads and chatty girls who didn't care to listen attentively or to behave cooperatively. The classmates resented our hero here, especially when the teacher would pronounce his name as a model which she wished we all would follow. Several weeks of such praising gathered into some very disagreeable teasing or sheer avoidance of that central character. One day, immediately following an occasion of teacher heralding the one exemplary person, he raised his hand and rose to say, "Miss X, I wish you would not speak of me in that way. I refuse to be marked as an outstanding member of this class any longer." He sat down and bowed his head perhaps as a humble apology to his peers. I think he resented being exploited by the teacher's weaknesses, her inability to find and meet the pupils where they were and to make contact first on their grounds and home base. Her failures had provoked measures of opposition and sabotage. Her further confrontations increased the resistances of the classmates and compounded them as is the case with iatrogenic complications in psychotherapy. Confrontation is inappropriate for the richer flow of exchange in educational and therapeutic relating.

If the envious classmates had confronted the teacher's favorite pupil directly, he would likely be subject to a variety of attacks and abuse. His immature status would force him to distort his functioning to be on better terms with his peers or otherwise complicate his autonomy and self expression. Perhaps such ramifications are realistically relevent to child psychotherapy. The adult patient, essentially self sufficient in ordinary social terms, could more safely avert peer pressures of this nature. If he is sufficiently mature he could also ward off even manipulative friendliness, seductive manoeuvers which conceal the aggressive envy, of those who might compliment him for his superior skill, his good fortune in having better sources or favorable connections and lucky encounters in life. He may welcome the elements of friendliness in these recognitions, but he can best return the compliment by wishing the others the opportunities for their own good experiences.

Thus, the therapist, often given positive regards for real or transferential qualities, will turn his attention and the patient's to the latter's hopes and efforts for his own advances. To simply or primarily confront the patient with interpretations about envy, projections of superior feelings or destructive maneuvers, impedes the working alliance. If the analyst moves the patient to make further efforts for himself, and if that fails, the patient may turn to his ally and ask for help to understand. Then the helper can offer tentative hypotheses about internal images and compromises instead of charging "resistance."

Since most of my orthodox-trained colleagues resist my position here, quoting their "Freud" emphatically, I was reas-

126

sured that my view was not so unique or extreme when I came on these sentences from Kohut's *How Does Analysis Cure* (1984, p. 173):

> Here, I would give voice to the opinion that the "confrontation" to which analysts expose their analysands not only are often trite, superfluous, and experienced as patronizing by the patient, but also may repeat the essential trauma of childhood in a way that is especially harmful to the progress of the analysis. By failing to acknowledge the validity and legitimacy of the patient's demands for development-enhancing selfobject responses, that is, the analyst fails the patient in the same way the parent had failed. . . .

However, Kohut then adds the following:

> That it may occasionally be helpful to an analysand, especially in the later phases of analysis, to hear from the analyst that old grievances, however valid and legitimate, must finally be relinquished, and that new and more responsive selfobjects must be sought in the present, goes without saying.

Here Kohut beings to intrude and presume in ways I find belittling to the patient's self-measure, self-regulation and his capacity to perhaps find and create his own best defenses for his still deeply private and subjective forces. Kohut here is making premature closures and preventing surprises.

I do recognize a significant impact of Self Psychology in the direction of Balint's clinical thinking. "The analytic atmosphere has become different" Kohut reports (1971, p. 157). Gustafsen (1976) suggests Balint and Kohut are complementary in that the latter encourages the idealizing transference while the former also does less interpretation but seeks to provide an attuning harmony in the relationship. Balint does prefer silent empathic understanding and recognition over active verbalizing. Yet Kohut assures us that " . . . the essential technique of analysis has remained unaltered . . . " (1971, p. 156). His message remains ambiguous; works like "technique" or "essential" become fuzzy; it becomes necessary to consider the details in attending to the subjectives and ethical experiencing, as I have been attempting.

Is it a purist position to question Kohut's presuming to advise the patient to relinquish a feeling of complaint? Is it an ethical pronouncement, or a temperamental preference, or simply a therapeutic principle? Can we distinguish these alternatives with any useful precision? If the patient invites us to make a measure of the validity of his complaining, or of any feeling, we could reflect back the wish that we "help" him to make closures or to continue protesting; a friendly neutral attitude may stimulate his further reflection and refinement of his private subjectivities. If he feels we are being inhuman in our response, we can indicate modestly that we really can't know as well as he might. Our humbleness here feels more honest and more respectful of his exploratory and creative possibilities. The patient may at first resent and "resist" our 'evasiveness.' Such 'resistance' seems appropriate to his taking more charge of his life actions; at least it is not a resistant response to our imposing confrontations or our playing presumptious, authoritarian roles.

With his human limitations, the therapist may feel he cannot afford emotionally to let the patient struggle on so he decides that the patient cannot afford to continue grappling with the issue, perhaps more so for female therapists. Parental attitudes do influence many of us in our professional work. And perhaps younger therapists may tend to be more confrontive, since youth is generally more ready to battle on for bolder solutions; culture, gender and sexual influences also operate. The many variables at work might be recognized in the characterological reactions to the patient's appeals or confrontations, but an ideal principle may be identified. Might we best be ready to spell out the alternatives evoked in us, when asked, for our tentative hypotheses—among which the patient may choose, rather than fight or resist us? The recent volume on *Resistance* (Milman and Goldman, 1987) presents sixteen viewpoints, historic and current, on these issues; only Greenson approaches the boldness of Gill's advances which are closest to the perspective I am putting forth. Gill too relieves the professional of the responsibility for regulating the frequency of sessions, the use of the couch and the diagnostic measure of illness (1988).

In summary, I see resistance analysis as wasteful, and harmful to the working alliance. It suppresses the open exploring of hidden feelings and fantasies. Its forms of confrontation, however subtle and seductive, violate the constructive potentialities of feeling in charge and responsible for one's measures and decisions in living. Resistance analysis decreases the prospects that the patient, and therapist, will experience the reflective autonomy and responsive intimacy which would signify positive therapeutic relating. Freud's short summary of the negotiation processes is: "The analyst agrees upon a fixed regular hour with the patient, gets him to talk, listens to him, talks to him in his turn and gets him to listen." (S.E. XX p. 187) Perhaps his clearest pointer against the principle of resistance analyses is his warning, in the same year he wrote his papers on technique, that "Analysis is not suited, however, for polemical use: it presupposes the consent of the person who is being analyzed . . . " (S.E. XIV. p. 49)

X

Surprising Echoes in New Resonances

It became puzzling to me that masochism, dream interpretation and resistance analysis remained cardinal in Reik's writings alongside the thesis of open exploring and self determination for the patient. I felt some contradictions and so came to review my total relationship to his ideas and his values. I found some answers.

The last time I met with Theodor Reik was in 1954. It was during his summer vacation at a large hotel upstate New York and he had invited me to spend a weekend at the hotel with him. We took many walks in the woods nearby and for the most part Reik talked about his life and his life-work, always looking backwards to Vienna as the glorious time and place. He spoke of his personal and professional ambitions as essentially unfulfilled. He said he still had dreams about writing more and more books and then tying them tightly into a bundle and hurling them at the father of his first wife. Reik offered the interpretation that he was wishing to give evidence of his worthiness to be given the beautiful bride, but that he now dared to show his anger to the father for pressuring him to prove himself. I was mostly silent on our walks, but I listened very intently to the heroic but sad image he was presenting. Reik hardly asked me about myself, though I had known him for ten years and in a variety of roles, originally as the reviewer of his first American book in 1944, then as a very enthusiastic and deeply moved reader of his most important book ever, *Surprise and the Psychoanalyst*.

Reik had suggested that I get in touch with him when I was released from military service. In late 1946, I became his analysand, although I had started training at the New York Psychoanalytic Institute. In 1948 Reik "graduated" me; it was a "surprising" analytic experience. Then he began supervising my first analytic case. I continued taking seminars in other Institutes in New York City and also began a new, more satisfactory analysis in 1950 with M. Barinbaum, as discussed in the previous chapter. Many questions about the gaps between theory and practice concerned me. In December 1948, Reik had invited me to join a small group of psychoanalysts who were meeting with him to plan for the establishment of the National Psychological Association of Psychoanalysis (NPAP). The group met at least once a week to work out the operating details of the new Institute and then of the Society for members and graduates. It was an exciting, defiant time, forced by the ideological rigidities of establishment Institutes. Under these circumstances, I was asked to teach the basic seminars on Freud's writings as well as those on Developers and Deviants of Psychoanalysis, each year, from 1950 to 1955,—a very stimulating period. It required a continual rethinking of our theories and methods; within six years I began to formulate the principles of my "ethical" approach (Shor, 1961).

Once the NPAP began to function, Reik withdrew and began to write more books, now less theoretical or conceptual, but full of his personal reminiscences and in a more purely literary style. His Ph.D. had been in the field of literature, in his early twenties; his dissertation, on Flaubert as psychologist, gained him Freud's appreciation. After 1952, I saw Reik accepting isolation from the general field of psychoanalysis but returning to his first love, his glorious Viennese literature, art and music. It may be that if his medical colleagues had been more friendly and ready to invite him to participate in dialogue as an equal member, Reik might have continued to contribute to psychoanalytic theory. He might have stopped his bad dreams of failure and angry revenge.

Yet, for me, his book, *Surprise and the Psychoanalyst*, remains as significant and relevant today as it was fifty years ago. I believe it is still ahead of our times. That book was written about 1934 in German and was translated and published in England and in the USA in 1937. I first heard of it in 1944, when I met Reik. I had reviewed his book, *The Psychologist Looks at Love*, for the American Psychological Association and I sent a reprint to Reik, who was already living in New York City. He was pleased with my mostly favorable review and invited me to his home. There, he gave me a copy of the *Surprise* book and our friendly association began. This book has been out of print for decades and is still difficult to find, even in analytic libraries. The explanation is in part very simple. Much of the text has been re-worked; it had been Americanized in 1948 and then incorporated into Reik's perhaps most popular and famous book, *Listening with the Third Ear*. Public responsiveness confirmed, for me, the validity of its ethical implications that the experiencer, the patient, is the best judge for depth psychology, ultimately and is entitled to know the therapist's professional assumptions.

I have made a comparison of the two books, *Surprise and the Psychoanalyst* and *Listening With the Third Ear*, in search of the basic themes which moved and inspired me so profoundly forty years ago. And I will try to point up their significance for the major trends in psychoanalysis as I see them today. For example, it is explicit that Reik, in his *Surprise* book, was primarily intent on investigating the theme of "the conjecture and the comprehension of unconscious processes." In the Americanized version, *The Third Ear*, the aim was put more loosely as a report on "the inner experience of a psychoanalyst." There is more theory for the psychoanalyst in the first version; there are more case illustrations and generalized literary comment for the intelligent layman in the second. Yet both are full of ideas about unconscious communication in all human relationships.

Let me take a leap to the very current scene in our field. I find most exciting the recent developments around the concept of empathy and subjectivity as they begin to be explored within the psychoanalytic process of therapy and in the observation of infants, as well as in all later stages of growth and maturation. I suggest that Reik's ideas about unconscious communication are richly relevant to our new concerns with dialogue processes in psychoanalytic therapy because of the new evidence for primary communication processes of resonance and attunement from birth onwards.

I want to trace the lines of communication, the bridges between "unconscious communication" and "dialogue", as they influenced my development as a psychoanalyst into the seemingly infinite and ever emerging fathoms of human communication. It is this aim which made the field of psychoanalysis so attractive for me from adolescence on. I experienced Freud's style of writing as personal and empathic, and so respectful of one's private processes of thinking and feeling.

So I begin with the period just before I met Reik as a backdrop for my present appreciation of his values. I had been working as an assistant to Ernst Kris for four years, for his seminars on psychoanalysis at the New School for Social Research and for his research projects on communication under the Rockefeller Foundation. To be working with Kris, a leader among the analysts of Freud's last circle in Vienna and in London, was very exciting and stimulating to that young clinical psychologist. I was allowed to hear and to discuss the emerging ideas about ego psychology as they reshaped the classical concepts in Freud's metapsychology. These theoretical reformulations seemed so crucial though highly intellectual. I lacked the clinical experience and the personal maturity to be fully comprehending of all I heard. My own experience in academic clinical psychology seemed somewhat distant, with only slight hints of the complexities being discussed abstractly. I knew I would need full formal training before I could appreciate the deeper implication of the theories for the practice. It was wartime and I was encouraged to hope that as soon as I was freed from military service I might be allowed to get training at the New York Institute.

I was accepted in 1946 and began training. I had seminars in the basics from Kris, Hartmann, Loewenstein and Spitz. The American Psychiatric Association then forced non M.D.'s out of the program and so I left. I refused to sign that I would never practice nor ever call myself a psychoanalyst. Yet my reading of Reik's *Surprise* book in 1944 had planted seeds which set me on a course and in a style of professional development which eventually moved me away from those classical, orthodox analysts. The lessons and lasting ideas in Reik's work were being internalized and my identification with his spirit, as I saw it or made it up, served to encourage or accentuate a highly individualistic quality even for the acquiring of training in psychoanalysis. That same spirit in fact also moved me later to leave Reik when he ignored my particular lines of interest in the field. Yet the central ideas in his book have reminded, underground, and I want to review and renew them and make some bridges to the ideas and methods which have become most important to me now, more than thirty years away from Reik.

There are many Freuds and there are many Reiks. We each create the images we seek. By 1950, when the NPAP began to function as an Institute, the official or orthodox analysts had hardened Freud's view into a fairly mechanistic system of drives and energies and into a formal, benignly authoritarian method of therapy much like the old medical model. It is to the credit of Ernst Kris and his colleagues (Hartmann, Loewenstein, Spitz, et al) that a breath of fresh air was beginning to be allowed in. They developed a comprehensive perspective for the Ego, calling it a "home defense department" with capacities for "autonomous functions" which permitted flexible adaptations and even creativity. These ideas are forerunners of what is now recognized as the importance of "safe space," as Winnicott has developed it. Beyond security, Kris was boldest with his formulation, "Regression in the Service of the Ego."

Spitz spoke more gently about the experiencing of affects, such as "the six month smile at the appearance of another human being" (1957). Spitz was beginning to study the earliest expressions and consequences of the dialogue in human growth and evolution. But his colleagues were not ready to have dialogues with *his* new ideas.

Reik had, earlier, in the *Surprise* book, speculated about the processes of instinctual resonance as unconscious communication among animals and in archaic "pre-civilized" humanity. But Reik's main contribution, I think, was the illumination and sounding of the variable pathways of such private and symbolic communication between highly civilized and sophisticated persons, as in the analytic relationship. He was ahead of his colleagues in this arena but he failed to attend sufficiently to the bridges that were needed. Some colleagues, like Kris, might make excursions in to primary processes, as in art or dreams. Reik married his ideas about unconscious communication. But he was seen and criticized as getting lost in this darker realm and becoming too mystical. As a dedicated artist, Reik risked much with his unexplained intuitions and his honesty about lacking systematic comprehension of the processes he glimpsed. He sought to relieve the therapist of authoritarian posing in his concluding chapter (1937) favoring "the courage not to comprehend". I began to see the dangers of *aiming* to understand the patient instead of allowing a sensitive relating with negotiation and empathy.

Reik made no secret about his battling with the establishment, perhaps all establishments. He sometimes wrote reassuringly that he recognized that his emphasis on the earlier intuitive phases of communication was preliminary and prerequisite to the rational, logical working through and working over of surprises for everyday living. He called on us to have more "moral courage", for inner "truthfulness." He alerted us to the subtle signals and cues which may signify an emerging message from the unconscious. He encouraged great patience and much silence in our practice. His messages have been mostly ignored by other analysts, or dismissed as heroics with irresponsible inactivity. Some of us saw his approach as an extreme respect for the private pace of exploring one's unconscious processes.

It leaves open the question, "*When* is it appropriate to intervene?" I propose that we try to offer tentative hypotheses for the complaints we sense being expressed or implied when the patient signifies he wishes us to know that he is unable to proceed in the self-management and self-analysis we both anticipate he will develop. We can learn to read his pauses also as possible invitations for empathy or for an interpretation. Thus, we negotiate a psychoanalytic dialogue in which the patient has the last word. With this point of view, I felt the freedom to make my own connections in the professional community and I believed that Reik respected my independence to explore.

I've come to think of Reik's conceptual and expressive boldness as his style of playfulness though perhaps without "sufficient" safe space in the profession. But he made his subjective measures of the risks and of the pains and pleasures, and he acted on his private decisions even in the face of unpredictable and predictable public consequences. His artistic passions seemed to permit such risky playfulness with his personhood and with his professional position.

For a short period I imitated this bold style in my own directions. I gathered the cues from *my* Freud about Thanatos, "the silent partner in the psyche," from Ferenczi and about "forced phantasies." I listened to the rumblings in and about Wilhelm Reich and made a friend and colleague of Alexander Lowen, the last psychotherapist trained by Reich, another iconoclastic, passionate devotee of his private convictions. I asked my Institute, the NPAP, to listen to Lowen on Bioenergetics—and to help try to make some bridges. Instead, Reik, with a sufficient percentage of NPAP members voted to ask me to leave, in 1955, for what I considered as my playful explorations. Reik had discussed such problems of "heresy" in an early book on *Myth, Dogma and Compulsion*. Now, Reik suddenly appeared to pronounce his official judgement against a colleague's differing investigations; despite ten years of fairly regular association, he never asked me anything about my interests in exploring Bioenergetics.

Reik here revealed the vulnerability of his own position, of exploring unconscious communication without sharing a sufficiently safe space. Reik's failure to develop a dialogue with me thus alerted me to my next needs for professional development in psychoanalysis. Yet I felt a deep sadness that Reik would not, did not, engage me in discussion to share my interests and explorations in or near psychoanalysis. He was not willing to dialogue beyond his own concerns about unconscious communication. And perhaps our walks in the woods of the Adirondacks less than a year previously were his offer of an explanation of the personal, unfinished ambitions which kept him unready, preoccupied and dedicated to the magical and symbolic qualities of literary self-expression. Though I lost all contact with him after his sudden authoritarian stance towards me, in 1955, I held on to the central ideas of his *Surprise* book and went searching for colleagues who would exchange and share more freely. The wish, the illusion of flexible dialogue, was still haunting.

The mysteries of the mind-body problem were equally enticing. My excursion into Bioenergetics with Lowen had such promise at first. I heard his enthusiasms for Wilhelm Reich's classical work on *Character Analysis* and the challenges to help the person re-open the hidden, loaded, locked up realms of experience in the body ego and in the non-verbal character traits. I enjoyed Lowen's speculations about the secret meanings in the silent expressiveness of muscular tonus. He heard my ruminations about the body ego as forerunners of the later, more developed "home defense department" (Kris) and about the likely qualities of crisis, shock, and surprise (Reik) at each step of self-liberation. He seemed to appreciate my selective references to the basic literature of psychoanalysis and its recognitions of next tasks for psychoanalysis, especially as we found these open ended issues in the writing of Freud, Ferenczi, and even Fenichel. After two years of friendly discussions, we agreed to write a book together, about 1957. And Lowen planned to organize an Institute for teaching his methods. I measured my degree of conviction about his techniques and I refused to be a founding partner, but I did agree to teach the history of psychoanalysis and also the explore its promising heritage for ongoing research. Lowen accepted my compromise position and we continued our joint efforts.

As I wrote drafts of chapters for the book we planned and started to teach in his Institute, we each began to recognize a central difference between us. The issue was the appreciation and respect for transference manifestations. I insisted on these deeply private and subjective aspects which made movement in psychotherapy unpredictable to a significant degree. This attitude followed closely from the Freud I valued and especially from Reik's *Surprise* book. I felt Lowen was impatient about the silences, both in the patient and in the therapist. He favored the direct approach of Wilhelm Reich and he pressured and argued seductively with the patient to submit to the therapist's active suggestions of physical, muscular provacations against the characterological "resistances" *he* pronounced. I said that this was too intrusive. Lowen had turned Reik's thesis about surprises inside out by justifying *his imposing* sudden surprises, even physical shocks on the patient and then apologizing sweetly that it was "necessary" for him to "break through." In his Institute Case Conferences, I pointed to his patient's submissiveness and self-devaluation under such practices. I worried out loud about the forced idealizations and the latent hostility and aggressiveness from these procedures. Lowen seemed to reach the limits of his tolerance for my questions about transference consequences and about the unexplored, unexpressed aspects of the whole patient-therapist relationship. This led to our separation. Our book did not continue.

I would not give up what I valued especially in Reik's themes about patience, silences and respect for the person's self-regulation. The next chapter will consider some further consequences of my efforts here to explore the mind-body links within the context of proper analytic values. Here my concerns were for more than the processes of transference, though I certainly accepted its central significance for evoking deeper dynamics in therapy, and perhaps I valued transference data even more explicitly than did Reik in his *Surprise* book.

Reik admitted to the view that "the analyst does come to his investigations with certain psychological assumptions and expectations" (p. 87) but he hardly elaborated this thesis and he failed to state or explore his own assumptions for our consideration as colleagues. Again I saw his valuable descriptions of unconscious communications and of the inner experience of conjecturing as needing a larger context. I needed more tentative hypotheses about the whole relationship of dialoguing between two essentially and potentially self-responsible, self-respecting persons in a process of selective sharing. The surprises Reik observed and experienced in himself and in his patient were *assumed* to be worked through and absorbed in the later phases of rational comprehension, after the earlier conjectures arose from echoes and rhythmic reverberations. Perhaps Reik had more trust in the human capacities to spontaneously assimilate one's own shocks into logical realistic actions, once the surprise is experienced. Perhaps he took the transference analysis for granted as established and more easily performed.

I then had been practicing analysis for about eight years. And during my training, Reik frequently consoled and reassured me, saying: "The first ten years of practice are the most difficult." It seemed I needed a teacher who would be more explicit and discuss his larger assumptions about the therapeutic interactions and yet one who would not abandon the spirit of sensitive patience and openness to surprise at depths, which Reik inspired.

My search was ongoing and I found my next model and teacher. It was Michael Balint whose first book, *Primary Love and Psychoanalytic Technique*, in 1952, engaged me with an excitement fully equal to that I had felt for Reik's *Surprise* book in 1944. I started a correspondence with Balint at once and he responded with a friendly interest in my questions and in my own suggestions of theory and method. I was delighted to learn that he was the literary executor for Ferenczi's manuscripts and yet was accepted as a training analyst for the British Psycho-analytic Institute. And especially significant to me were the facts that he had been trained primarily by Ferenczi and yet had, as early as in 1932, published that firm critique of Ferenczi's activity experiments in psychoanalytic methods. Balint seemed to echo a central note of Reik's approach in his pointed observation:

> That is the crucial point: that the amount of excitation the degree of tension, is actually determined by the patient himself. This explains why in many cases the otherwise useful interventions (such as those recommended by Ferenczi) remain ineffectual.

This statement by the young Balint was made at the same time Reik was preparing his *Surprise* book. But Balint lived and worked in London.

London was far away to me at that time. I was very much a native New Yorker who believed it was the center of the world, the only place for great heroic accomplishments and stimulation. I tried to be open to all the varied and contradictory resources at hand. I felt the American culture was the promise for the future of humankind. I think some of us still believe that. Back in the 1950's, I ventured to approach all the possibilities for stimulation in the complex New York psychoanalytic scene.

Yet the image of British culture, in London, was highly idealized in my mind as the most mature civilization in human history and the most respectful of private individual developments and idiosyncracies. I had experienced these qualities in my relationship with Kris, who shared these values. I felt this idealization from British political history and its heritage of literature, science and social customs, especially when visiting in London. I read this vision for open-ended evolution in Freud's frequent comment that *London* is the true home of psychoanalysis, not Vienna, nor Berlin, nor New York, and I heard this idealized view of London in occasional remarks by my father, though he had never been there. That special image of London, where Balint lived, haunted me all through the 1950's and I scouted throughout the rich reservoirs of professional competition and the sometimes insidious tensions, among the offerings in New York City. Yet I did think that Reik had chosen New York City, and not London, as a more dramatic stage for his self-expression.

Balint's correspondence was very affecting, both in its style and its content. He wrote in a spirit of interplay between two persons each offering their private explorations and considerations. When I had lost Reik and then felt the New York scene too full of competitive tension, it will not surprise you that I responded affirmatively to Balint's suggestion in 1960 that I move to London and join the staff and faculty of the Tavistock Clinic and Institute.

I want to believe that if I had discussed my decision with Reik and with Kris, there would have been a renewal of interest and friendliness about the "hunches" (a term Kris frequently used) and the "conjectures" (Reik's favorite idea) which I was pursuing. At least, I imagine their silent attention to my new interests in aspects of psychoanalysis which may not have been at the center of their own formulations. I want to assume that a deep level of psychic similarity is available to us all to allow any communication. Reik was often explicit in his *Surprise* book (pp. 19+, 59+, 123+, 195+, 233+, 250+) about the basic psychological unity at the depths of us all:

> Now the unconscious functions alike in everybody as an organ for seizing upon the concealed processes in the inner life of other. It has the same tendencies and the same methods of work. (p. 264)

This unifying thesis is an hypothesis necessary, I think, for pursuing the project of psychoanalytic therapy yet it needs an elaboration. We must start with the surface variations of individuals as they first present themselves. Reik recognizes this dimension in his quoting the French proverb, "The Style is the Man", and he even suggests that Freud has deepened the aphorism to state "the style is the history of the person." Yet Reik, in approaching a patient, seemed to choose a manner of extreme silence rather than to meet with the surface presentation or to develop a dialogue by sensitive negotiations. He fa-

141

vored incisive "inner truthfulness" rather than content with the variable complexities and obstacles to an outer or surface honesty. I found Reik's style of relating as a more difficult, perhaps more a challenging and heroic process than Balint's style. Balint began by meeting the surface and negotiating gradually to develop a safe space for self-reflection. Balint responded to the selective and self-paced openness for echoes and resonances within and from the other person. It was Balint's style that moved me to London in 1961.

I now can identify the specific turning point at which I decided to move. It was my recognition that Reik's profound insights into unconscious communication could be enriched and actualized by learning the manners of Balint's more comprehensive approach to the inner life of oneself and of the other.

In 1959, Balint published a daring and delightful little book, called *Thrills and Regressions*. This work is today still essentially neglected by his colleagues in the British Society and at large, much as Reik's *Surprise* book is ignored by psychoanalysts in general. Balint proposes that, along with other experiences at the beginning of life, we also have timeless moments of experiencing a "Primary Love", a constructive illusion of perfect harmony with our source. It was a kind of primary dialogue and a model for adult mutuality. I read into his hypothesis the idea that this image or prototype might remain at the deepest layers of the unconscious and serve as anchor, motivation and model for all subsequent human efforts for psychic and social developments, both individual and cultural. I could then see Spitz's well known reports and interpretations, in 1945 and 1946, about severely deprived infants with no experience of friendly mothering as confirmations, years in advance of Balint's proposal. Then his *Thrills* book proceeds to recognize the universal probability of some degree of failure, some occasions of imperfect harmony which stimulate either of two opposing basic styles of defensive adapting, yet with the still more basic hidden hope that the style chosen will someday yield or achieve a return to a fully successful "Primary Love." Balint names the opposing styles "ocnophilic" or a love for clinging for safety and supplies, and "philobatic" or a love for freedom and independent movement.

Balint admits the temptation to identify the clinging pattern as maternal and feminine in our culture and the philobatic as inventive, heroic and masculine, but he asks that we remain open to changes here. In contrast, I think many of us have heard about Theodor Reik's male chauvinist point of view. It was usually stated with charm and chivalry in the spirit of Viennese sophistication. Yet, Reik often told me that he thought psychoanalytic therapy was essentially a feminine function, for its attitude of caring for the patient in a gently and forebearing manner. However, he then would say that the psychoanalyst would need to restrain that caring attitude to encourage the person to feel free and bold in facing unconscious processes, to learn to be independent.

I very much appreciated Balint's interpretation of our usual orthodox, classical analytic procedures as reinforcing the clinging defense because of their rules and required techniques. Reik had long ago, in the 1937 *Surprise* book, expressed this opposition to the explicit modes of regulation by the analyst. I had responded resonantly to Reik's statements in 1944, fifteen years before I again appreciated the critique of the official rules of analysis in Balint's 1959 book. However, Balint proceeds to a further warning about a one-sided approach like Reik's, which was almost exclusively "quiet, undemanding, unexacting" in spirit. Balint writes:

> The greatest danger, to my mind, is that this technique may leave too much to the patient, forcing on him too much independence too early; this, then, in the same way as the ocnophilic (clinging) technique may lead to introjecting the aggressor, in this case the philobatic analyst as a demanding figure, exacting heroic standards from his poor patients. (*Thrills,* p. 106).

The larger implication, for me, is the advantage of flexible dialogue which allows open negotiations for creating a safe "atmosphere in which the patient feels free to focus on his inner self" (Shor, J. Int. J. Psychoan. V. 51, p. 247).

Balint's critique exposed, for me, the vulnerability of Reik's style: his heroic stance about his own life work, his imposition of unresponsive silences upon the patient to provoke a sense of drama and crisis in the hope of evoking an heroic spirit in the other. I began to feel that approach was manipulative, however benign the intent. It smacks of the resolute isolation and sense of rejection which permeates Reik's last chapters. It contains and conceals, I believe, his pessimistic feelings about society, about intimacy and loving, about the possibilities of any enriched or mature mutuality or dialogue in human evolution.

Reik finds compensation in that image of the creative hero all alone. All of these downbeat themes are undercurrents in several of Reik's last books. His statements are generally put with a charming Viennese sophistication which is the hallmark of that culture as it flowered and decayed so richly from the nineteenth century on into the early twentieth century. You may remember the report of my last talks with Reik on our walks in the countryside where he reminisced so sadly about the glorious life in Vienna, its dashing and daring inventiveness in art, music and literature, its medley of insights into the complex rhythms and resonances of the human psyche, and its delivery of Freud and his creation of psychoanalysis. It would seem that Reik never left that home, even though he did Americanize his magnificent book, *Surprise and the Psychoanalyst*, into a *Third Ear*.

But that is not the end of Reik's story. During his last fifteen years, he published a host of literary expressions, with *Haunting Melodies* and *Secrets* and *Fragments of a Confessions*. I see in these last works a supplicant reaching for acceptance back into a hoped-for newly friendly society, an admission of his weaknesses and vulnerabilities,—and a wish to transcend his lonely, heroic philobatic position in life, to renew a primary love which will also recognize *his* discoveries and contributions to the fuller life of us all. Well, when I could see Reik's life work and style in the larger and also safer context of Balint's fresh ideas about primary models for human development and for psychoanalytic method, I felt ready to leave New York and move to London.

XI

Self Provocation and Reparation

Before leaving New York City, I had to do some further sifting of the rich stimulation I had experienced there—the many other thinkers heard at the New School for Social Research (Horney, Fromm, Reich), the series of guests at the Federn Group (Bergler, Bunker, Waelder), the neo-Reichian groups (Lowen, Pierrokas), the Inter-personal school of Sullivanians (Clara Thompson, Fromm-Reichman, Maskin) and surely others. The themes of pre-oedipal and non-verbal processes and dynamics had been relatively neglected in the orthodox atmosphere of the New York Analytic Society, whose meetings I had continued attending.

Surrounding the Centennial of Darwin's *Origin of Species* (1856), much discussion about his life work appeared in professional and general intellectual publications. I was drawn to his work on *The Expression of Emotions* (1872), as closer to my experience with patients. Reading these books, I saw the challenge of differentiating the "normal" from the "neurotic" experiencing of bodily pains and complaints and so I proceeded to make a systemic study of patients under physiotherapy at the Roosevelt Hospital in Manhatten under a formal curriculum of the Swedish Institute of Psychotherapy and Massage. This six-month, quarter-time course served to show the continual overlap of patterns of complaining about private bodily experiences with the subtle variables of patients' attitudes about the relationship to the attending specialist. Of course, these clients were not in analysis and their "resistances" were not subject to analysis. My gross speculations needed some anchoring and I found this in Darwin's descriptions of emotions in expression. I also saw his implicit therapeutic principles about "recovering elasticity of mind" (1872, p. 365).

Armed with these new cues, I came to London and soon after presented a theoretical discussion on "Sources for Psychoanalysis in the Work of Darwin" to the London Imago Group. A friendly reception encouraged me to offer a more clinical paper to the British Psycho-Analytic Society on some links between Darwin's ideas and the main line of thought which was begun in the 1953 paper on "Ego Development Through Self Traumatization." My Society talk was much less effective in evoking interest, as Balint had predicted to me.

Only afterwards did I realize a possible reason for my failure. At the end of chapter seven, I suggest the explanation, the difference between Darwin's and Freud's attitudes about measuring private affect. I had ignored Balint's principle of critique of Ferenczi for not giving thorough priority to the patient's measure of his experience. My neglect left my message as allowing a presumptuous domination of the pacing and measure of the patient's feelings, which should be recognized as a self-regulative process in the subject. I had made Ferenczi's error.

Yet that unpublished paper did also include the first specific indications of my concern for modifying classical "technique" of psychotherapy as well as my first formulations of the practical applications of Freud's earliest theory of the components of instinct in humans, as opposed to lower animals. A further possibly significant idea in this presentation is the interpretation of "screen memories" (Freud, 1899) as cues to reparative wishes short-circuited by iatrogenic transferences. This theme was first noted in a 1953 publication (Coleman and Shor) on "Ego Development Through Self-Traumatization" and is developed to encompass the classical concept of repetition compulsion and the traditional phenomena of masochistic acting out; these orthodox views underlie the emphasis on resistance analysis. The transition is made here to the principle of priority for primary positive motivations in the details of clinical practice. Therefore I am presenting this 1963 paper for the British Psycho-Analytic Society in full text:

Self-Provocation and Reparation

In a previous publication ("Ego Development Through Self-Traumatization", *Psychoanalytic Review*, 1953) clinical examples were given of children provoking their parents to manifest hostile attitudes in the hope of externalizing these "bad objects" and thus achieving a clearer perspective for further ego defence. During analysis as adult patients, they came to learn how such provocations emerged from their unconscious dreads about their parents' unconscious attitudes. The provocative incidents had occurred between the ages of six and twelve years and were persistently recalled during treatment as justification for character weaknesses. These "screen memories" were repeated until the provocative aim was interpreted as a testing. Similar provocations were expressed in the transference; this time analysis permitted the patient to recall and reconstruct the reparative aims concealed behind the long-standing screen memories of these crucial traumatic events. In these cases the exposure of parental hostility had resulted in a fresh trauma too severe to allow the child then to recognize consciously his wish to repair the parent or to develop new ego defenses against external traumatization.

Another publication ("A Well-Spring of Psychoanalysis", *Psycho-analysis*, 1953) suggested that reparation is part of the aim of all creative activity including the usefully narcissistic aspects of a fuller maturity. When object relations fail, the reparative aim may include efforts to repair oneself, as well as the repairing of bad or destroyed objects. Character neuroses are especially likely to contain damaged body ego functions; these weaknesses may be bound up with layers of never verbalized dread about lasting damage to one's functions of instinctual expression. Here too, analysis may facilitate a process of self-provocation in the patient, so that he evokes in himself more of these anxieties obstructing his possession and use of deeper narcissistic resources.

Self-provocation is an experiment, a testing of reality, inner and outer reality. When the provocation fails to allow a working through to a better position for ego defence, the attempt has usually been called a "repetition compulsion" or a "masochistic acting out;" both terms have been identified as expressions of Freud's Death Instinct. A successful self-provocation will lead to the relinquishing of a bad introject and the establishing of a stronger narcissistic phase, in preparation for a better pattern of object relationship. In this sense, a successful self-provocation is a constructive acting-out. The consciously self-directed acting-out may yield a discharge of anxiety about an instinctual component and allow the patient to make a clearer measure of his pain and pleasure, and their origins. Such knowledge equips the ego for a more precise management of its sources and resources, and fosters the spiral of creative and flexible ego development.

It remains to be demonstrated in clinical experiences that such self-provocative procedures within treatment may escape the pitfalls of transference indulgence and split-off discharges of feeling. One remembers the recurrent controversy about the question of acting-out in the experiments of Ferenczi, Reich, and other analysts.

The process of self-provocation has in fact always been in the nature of the therapeutic workings of transference analysis. Anna O. literally insisted upon Breuer's patient attendance according to her pace and measure of tension, and she thus initiated the psycho-analytic situation and its particular ethic, ("The Ethic of Freud's Psycho-Analysis," Int. J. Psyoan, 1961). The further progress of analytic method and theory depends upon the continued insistence of our patients and their demands for deeper self-knowledge.

My last six years of analytic practice in New York City provided me with the opportunity to work with a number of such insistent patients, people with more than eight or ten years of previous analytic treatment. Amongst these were several valid complainers who pressed for more opportunity for deeper levels of self-provocation. They presented themselves as having character difficulties for which previous analytic insight proved helpful but insufficient for satisfactory change. These experienced patients were the clinical stimuli to certain explorations into the extension of routine character analytic method when demanded by patients.

Working with such persistent patients may sometimes allow one to speculate about the correctness of previous therapy. Such speculations are at best private guesses burdened with many unverifiable interpretations.

The theoretical stimuli to my explorations in method of treatment emerged from the history of Freud's efforts to find the clinical implications of his speculations about the Death Instinct. Also specially stimulating were certain works of Ferenczi, "On Forced Fantasies" and on Relaxation Techniques, Reich's *Character Analysis*, and Balint's writings on "The New Beginning". Complementary to these sources, Charles Darwin's book, *The Expression of the Emotions in Man and Animals* offered general principles and specific suggestions of method for deepening the study of unity and splits in body-mind (affect-idea) expressions of "nerve-force".

The three types of crisis are derived directly from the three aspects of the instinct:

deprivation of primary narcissistic supplies—instinctual *source*

suppression of expressive functions (body-ego)—instinctual *aim*

frustration of discharge into external reality—instinctual *object*

Clinical examples will be given of the characteristic complaints corresponding to each of these types of ego failure. My original analytic training in New York was within the tradition of instinct theory, and I hope to show this aspect to be still useful within object relationship therapy.

149

The work of Mrs. Klein includes the development of our insight from the concept of reparation for a wide range of normal and pathological processes of object-relationship. The concept of self-provocation may add to this approach if it results in clinical methods and data bearing on the reparation of faulty narcissistic processes, such as damaged body ego aspects of instinctual expression. Also it may offer cues for differentiating more precisely the experience of deprivation (oral phase) from that of frustration (phallic-hysteric phase).

Recent work by Bowlby ("Processes of Mourning", Int. J. Psyoan., 1961) includes observations and concepts about the phases of mourning which appear to correspond to the three aspects of an instinct. If so, one may relate his data on the sense of loss in physical separation and death to a wider range of obstructions to good (genital, mutual) object-relationships. (End of pre-circulated introduction, held as read.)

Mr. Chairman, Members, and Guests,

I wish to thank the society for the opportunity to present these research notions for discussion.

From the American scene, one has come to recognize as the hallmark of the English school the intensive analysis of the transference, and surely this is the central idea of psycho-analysis. There have been certain developments in American psycho-analysis which may be viewed as wanderings from the home base. But some of these forays into theory and experiments with method may be parameters which can come to find a place within the scope of the full-bodied development of object-relations theory and method for therapy.

My entire professional experience until 1961 was in N.Y.C., where I was trained within the tradition of Instinct theory, mostly under supervision by members of the New York Psycho-Analytic Society. In 1950, Mrs. Klein's writings had begun to appear in book form, and I became interested in discussing her major concepts with my colleagues. It was striking how difficult it was to gather together a small private seminar group, and how the neglect of Mrs. Klein's work among the New York analysts persisted through the 1950's. There seemed little interest in exploring the richness of her concept of reparation, or in examining her formulations about the depressive and paranoid positions in early development.

The United States has produced much other experimentation and speculation with analytic method and theory, but these new developments have frequently resulted in the formation of new groups and training institutes, each one acting independently, and in apparent isolation from the others. This phenomena of competitive group formation is, in fact, fairly typical of American Society; just as it is a general cultural trend to discourage the manifestations of depression. There is little public acceptance of sadness, of silence or of privacy. The emphasis is upon promiscuous, manic friendliness, with a denial of depressive and paranoid ideas and feelings. One is tempted to speculate further about the cultural differences between English and American psychoanalysis. But I would rather report certain exploratory clinical procedures in my practice during the second half of the 1950's.

The phenomena of the persistent patient had become fairly widespread. These were the people who continued seeking analytic help after as much as 10 years of previous treatment, whether with one or several therapists, and possibly from a variety of analytic training institutes. These people were sampling and exploring the variety of new approaches in search of more satisfactory therapeutic "success" *according to their own definitions*. Many of these patients could not be dismissed simply as schizoid or narcissistic characters, and they may be viewed, not as "failures", but as a challenge to current clinical practice.

It remains an open question whether these experienced patients would be satisfied by a fuller analysis of the early depressive and paranoid phases of their development. Some differences in theoretical formulation have been known to conceal basic similarities in methods of treatment. In view of this, I would like to present some clinical procedures in my attempts to meet the demands of these experienced patients, from the point of view of Instinct theory.

There were among these persistent patients many who

could be called "valid complainers". They had benefited significantly from correct, good, analytic practice, but still wanted more complete satisfaction and fulfillment for themselves. These veteran patients were realistic about the boldness of their complaint, and in their attitude to previous therapeutic experiences. They presented themselves as having character difficulties on which they had been working, but they found they were "stuck", blocked in their analytic treatment, which had become "stagnant". For example, they identified their specific difficulties in experiencing and expressing assertive or tender feelings in constructive ways. They recognized many fantasy complications which had long disturbed their work and love relations. Most typically they complained of an inability to feel completely the analytic ideas and interpretations which seemed so correct and clarifying.

The terms of their complaints were usually put in words such as these: I was helped by Dr. X or Dr. Y. I came to understand the neurotic basis of my symptoms, I learned my defenses. I became able to spot these neurotic processes very easily and I could *stop* myself from *repeating* them. Sometimes I could force myself to try to respond in a new way; but mostly I was busy being *aware* of my complications . . . I want to be able to take all this insight for granted and really live more spontaneously, without so much introspection".

These "valid complainers" were not psychotic and they were not being supported by inherited or family funds. They generally carried on conventionally adequate work histories and sometimes marriages too, and they spent hard-earned money in order to continue their analytic search. Although for some, symptoms persisted, they reported that they were much less desperate; but they still wanted "more out of life".

Some of these people had ventured into non-analytic approaches, which included various philosophical, quasi-religious and physio-therapeutic practices. But finding these failed for them, they returned to analysis where they came to re-examine their failure to achieve *central* gains from these explorations; they were able to analyze out the magical elements in these therapeutic practices, and spoke sadly about their failure. Still, these experienced, analytic patients reported that they had achieved *glimpses* of hope for reparation and they wished that analysis with its more fundamental framework could find a way to incorporate these glimpses. These people were the practical pressure and stimulus that led me to attempt to extend regular character analytic treatment through methods of self-provocation.

There were also many theoretical stimuli to experimentation with the method of treatment: the hints in Freud's writings about studying body sensations and the musculature for applying his speculations about the death instinct, the suggestions and experiments by Ferenczi, the formulations in Wilhelm Reich's *Character Analysis*. I also found cues in the investigations by Fenichel into psychosomatic symptoms, in his writings of the late 1920's. One could extend the list of sources but I would like to suspend the question of theory until after we examine the practical clinical procedures of self-provocation with their new complications of the transference.

I think we would agree that the routine practice of character analysis is very variable, at least as variable as the making of interpretations about purely verbal associations. In both types of clinical intervention, each of us makes his decisions about timing, about the amount of detailed evidence brought to bear, and about the style of expressing our interpretative insight. Yet there is no variance about the principles that guide our basic approach.

Throughout I have tried to maintain the classical principle that the criterion of properly evoked feelings is the appearance of fresh free-associations which contain that mixture of fantasy and reality data—which is then to be sorted out. The process of working-through the new data verbally remains the central criterion of our analytic offering; its success is measured by the effective recall or reconstruction of "the fragments of historical truth" (Freud 1937) as the kernel of reality at the base of the trauma. The procedures I have tried are parameters of classical method and as such, it was important to keep the classical principles in mind.

My first step beyond the traditional method was to move my chair forward to be parallel to the patient's head, not behind him. Was this an intrusion upon the patient's private space for expressing his verbal associations? Or was it allowing the patient an easier choice about looking at me, or away from me? At least, I had the advantage that I could see more precisely the non-verbal details of his resistance.

The first new principle from Darwin for clinical procedure which I explored was: THE PRINCIPLE OF DELIBERATE EXAGGERATION OF THE EXPRESSIVE GESTURES.

When routine analytic interpretation of the transference appeared to be insufficient, the suggestion was made to the patient to try to express in a deliberate and exaggerated way the specific feeling which we had agreed was difficult for him to experience constructively. For instance, the patient who has come to know about his fear of asserting his proper authority may yet hold his jaw stiffly forward. All my efforts to relate this rigidity to the idea of hidden anger, as the unconscious response to the phantasies previously revealed in analysis, may still fail to evoke in him the recognition and experience of the feeling. He may want more freedom and flexibility in expressing such feelings in realistic and useful situations. I would recommend he try to deliberately assume an *angry* manner. Sometimes the fact of my suggestion alone has aroused his awareness of the hidden feeling, without any actual efforts of trying; and then the analysis proceeded along traditional lines. If we fail, I wait for a fresh complaint close to the same character difficulty. In case of success *or* failure, I look for the new transference-resistance complications from my having made a suggestion. For example, if the patient looked for my approval or my evaluation of his "performance", I interpreted this; and waited for a spontaneous renewal of his reparative wish for his own judgment of his capacity and satisfaction in self-expression of the hidden feeling.

My next step was to talk about muscles, not feelings. Instead of asking the patient to "make an angry face", I tell him to try to "make his jaw rigid, more than usual". As work proceeded, I added some details of the muscles involved in expression. This step applies the hypothesis that traumatic experience may leave a deposit of muscular rigidity in those organ systems which are usually employed in discharging the instinctual tension.

Patterns of muscle involvement in feelings were described in detail by Charles Darwin, in 1872, in his *The Expression of "Emotion in Man and Animals.* There he presents his three principles of expression. The first is "The principle of serviceable associated habits". This is the keynote to the current view that emotional expression is a state of incipient stimulation of the muscles appropriate to the intended action; the act is not completed and the undischarged "nerve-force" initially aroused remains bound in the expressive organs, or becomes available for innervating other body organs and muscular pathways. It is general meta-psychological speculation that conscious thought and feeling arise in this way. Clinical practices like the above exaggerating of gestures may explore the process of provoking in oneself a fuller awareness of previously hidden feelings. And then if the transference is properly analyzed out, the therapy can be advanced.

Sometimes, however, such deliberate exaggeration of expressive gestures failed to produce a clearer awareness of feeling, but rather evoked a new spate of resistance, overt or hidden. I would alert the patient to this new defense, and I interpreted this shift of resistance as further evidence of the workings of his character neurosis. When classical interpretation of the new resistance failed to move us on, I came to note that the new resistance had produced slight signs of expressive gestures which were directly opposite in muscle tonus, opposite to the characteristic expressions of the patient.

Charles Darwin offers a second principle of interpreting expression: *"The Principle of Antithesis".* He described "a strong and involuntary tendency to the performance of movements of a directly opposite nature, opposite to the usual habitual reaction, when a directly opposite state of mind is induced". This is clearly a process of defense. We now use the term "character trait" for his term "habitual action", and we speak of "resistance" to include his phrase "opposite state of mind".

The procedure that followed from Darwin's second principle, might be identified simply as: THE PRINCIPLE OF DELIBERATE EXAGGERATION OF THE OPPOSITE FEELINGS.

This clinical procedure evolved more slowly. For some patients my new suggestions served only to intensify their resistant attitudes; I interpreted this, and insisted that their stronger denials were further evidence for the correctness of my hypotheses. But as long as my patients refused to move, my interpretations remained useless speculations. However, I came to recognize that some of them actually had moved, though in a direction opposed to my suggestions. When I had made the special attempts to suggest and evoke the hidden feelings, and I paused, often feeling discouraged, the patient noticed this cessation of my efforts, and *I* noticed that his expressive manners changed strikingly at this point. For example, during my strong suggestions that he exaggerate the angry gestures, his usually firm jaw held forward with stiff shallow breathing, now dropped back becoming soft and reticent. If I remained silent a while longer, he slowly resumed his characteristically rigid jaw and chest. Another patient, with listless eyes and a usually crest-fallen posture which suggested helplessness and resignation, was asked to exaggerate his collapsed chest. He rather became stiff and alert until I ceased my efforts to intensify his weak feelings. Then he slowly resumed his characteristic posture.

Apparently my suggestions had provoked these patients to a defensive maneuver; they assumed expressive gestures directly opposing the hidden feelings which I tried to expose. I pointed this out as a hint of hidden capacity they had wanted, and I invited the patient to try deliberately to assume these opposite gestures. In preparation for these efforts, I reviewed the clinical evidence demonstrating that his usual character traits were obstructing him from realities and pleasures he wanted. He might argue and so I wait for a fresh transfer-

156

ence expression to illustrate the unrealistic distortion. Some patients came to agree and would renew their efforts. Others merely conceded that my hypothesis was a plausible idea, but were willing to experiment out of desperation. Still others would dismiss my speculation as useless, and stop working with me.

It was, of course, necessary to be alert to their manner of willingness or of resistance; this was sometimes a further expression of character defences and I would stop any of these experiments *to make the interpretation* of this transference character-resistance in the hope that this new piece of interpretation would allow the analysis to proceed without any further extensions of method. If this failed, I would renew my suggestion that he provoke himself in the specific ways opposite to his repressed feelings.

When some degree of cooperation was available, the self-provocation through muscle movements resumed; the patient sometimes protested against the "silly acting", or the "foolish gesturing". I reminded him he is free to refuse and stop at any point. If he adopted a stalemate position, I still offered to continue our working together if he wished it. If he remained, I asked him to focus as directly as possible on his feelings of complaint and discontent. I was pleased to see that this frank attitude could stimulate some of these experienced patients to a renewed search for reparation.

I then asked him to try again to exaggerate both his characteristic expressive gestures and then the opposite expressions. He often performed mechanically, holding his breath, or he playfully made expressions of varying forms of distortion, especially in his face. I interpreted those as attempts to swing free of my focused attention and so to keep his *feelings* concealed. If he tried again, he would experience his movement between the positions, and he could begin to feel the change in muscle tonus. He sometimes felt he was re-discovering the feeling of having a mobile chin, or shoulders, or a chest that could move, or hands that can touch with feeling, with precision, and with pleasure. My flexible attention to specific muscle actions was useful in awakening some new interest in

157

experiencing his body sensations and investigating their emotional contexts.

It was some time before we knew what to make of some of these data, the reports of "tingling", "streaming", and "quivering" sensations, and the observations of changing rhythms of breathing. These were either pleasant feelings of moving free of his usual limits or they were the strains and pains of his long-standing defensive muscle-bound state. For example, a patient usually feeling empty and collapsed, began to identify the heavy and pressed sensations in his abdomen, chest and neck. His new awareness of discomfort provoked efforts to attain release, and hopes for an experience of function-pleasure in assuming a more firm and alert posture.

When new feelings were aroused, the patient usually was pleased and more hopeful about our working together further. He would proceed to establish these new expressive patterns with me, and spontaneously in some of his difficult life situation outside; and he would report his successes and failures. As anticipated, the successes sometimes ran into failure because the infantile sources were not yet worked through systematically. These fresh failures, being nearer to the vivid sensations of the conflict, have sometimes succeeded in evoking spontaneous associations and memories about early traumata bearing on the specific character problem. We are then able to reconstruct in more detail the original processes of adopting the specific defenses. The character analysis is given the impetus of a more affective experience of the neurosis, through motivating the defenses with feeling, and liberating the elements of "historical truth" in the experiences of the traumata.

If there are any new degrees of success, they would derive from these new factors, even if they may complicate the task of analyzing the transference, because they are parameters: First, the fact that I had suggested to the patient ways of responding to his instinctual conflicts, ways which he had himself stopped daring, now revived the reparative wish to be able to express. The new experiences, first in session, later at his own choice, outside, yielded the second factor: from his exploring his sensations in session, he gained glimpses of feeling renewed hope, which helped to carry him through the expected cycles of slipping back to his old defensive position. Becoming familiar with failure, he was able to use this period for objective and calm awareness of his own defensive processes, especially through noting the ease or difficulty of his breathing.

The third factor of possible value from these experiments in self-provocation is the strong focus on a sharper awareness of the patient's reparative intent behind his defenses, rather than of the resistances alone. These three factors are risks in that they make necessary more busy-ness in the analysis of the transference; if this is done well enough, it may yield valuable gains for therapy and research.

Sometimes the results were less rewarding. The patient tried the opposite expressive gestures, then relaxed his muscles and felt the contrast as he resumed his characteristic manner; but the new awareness of this range of expression remained a distant, intellectual perception, an impersonal, mechanical feeling. In other cases the patient found the new efforts simply too painful; for example, he was unable to stretch his shoulder muscles without very great discomfort, and he would not proceed. There were those who refused to consider my suggestions and resented any comment about their gestures and expressions as untrue or as unnecessary intrusions. They demanded new ideas, new interpretations to explain and relieve their discontent. I attempted to interpret the elements of infantile, magical thinking in their demand for new ideas from inside me. If such interpretations failed, I, too, felt the need for a more comprehensive approach to the muscular involvements of character rigidity, more fundamental than the particular expressions of specific defense mechanisms. A variety of body sensations were reported and I felt the lack of an adequate language for these experiences and sensations. I am reminded of the research task implied in Freud's comment in 1923, in his *Ego and the Id,:* "The ego is first and foremost a body ego" and it "is ultimately derived from bodily sensations". And also his letter to Fliess, in 1899, in which he suggests, "From time to time, I visualize a second part of the method of treatment—provoking patient's feelings as well as their ideas, as if that were quite indispensible".

The two principles so far applied did yield a cue for a more systematic approach. When the patient would provoke himself by exaggerating the expressive behavior, and then by exaggerating the opposite expression, his pace of breathing changed, from inspiration to expiration, and vice versa. The tensing of muscles, for action of expression, would not be experienced as an emotional state until he expired and relaxed the specific muscles, at least to a degree. And if he sighed gently while breathing out, the awareness of the specific quality of feeling would be increased. Such parallel stimulation of his awareness of both the expressive intent and the accompanying feelings and sensations would allow fresh memories of and associations to the related traumatic situations.

Since sound making is the pathway to human speech, and breathing is the vehicle for the expression of emotions, there is a cue in this combined approach for a more systematic method of studying the interactions of feelings and ideas, of mind and body, within the process of analytic treatment.

Darwin offers as a third principle;—"The Principle of Direct Action of the Nervous System". Here he points to the difficulties in studying the mind-body relation. He speaks of the overflow of "nerve-force" into other parts of the neural system, an analogy which Freud used in first describing the split between feelings and ideas which we recognize is at the base of neurotic processes. Darwin also raises questions about the power and functioning of "attention", or "will", of "consciousness" in general, and he stressed the central role of breathing in permitting awareness of feelings. In speculating about the patterns of overflowing "nerve-force", Darwin suggested a sequence of expressive muscle systems which has some striking correspondences to the muscular layers of defenses as outlined by Wilhelm Reich, and some links to speculations by Fenichel in 1928 about "libidinalization" of body organs and variations in breathing, as defenses.

It would take us too far afield at this time to comment on

the theoretical implications of the work of early Reich and early Fenichel. I feel the need first to clarify the principles of method in character analysis. The principle of self-provocation can sharpen our attention to the three basic types of unresolved infantile traumata; *deprivation, suppression* and *frustration*. These types of ego failure are derived directly from the three phases of the instinct.

When Freud first formulated his Instinct Theory approach in 1905, in his "Three Contributions to the Theory of Sex", he differentiated the three aspects of the full development of an instinct: *Source, Aim* and *Object*. Of course he recognized there that all three aspects, that all human development, are uniquely bound within the context of object-relations; yet each aspect of the instinct produces a different quality and function in a relationship. The procedures of self-provocation may be used to focus the analysis upon these differences in ego function or failure.

Thus the term *Source* refers to the experience of being supplied with good feelings without the need for the sense of effort. The successful experience of a Source-relationship has been described in the analytical literature as "basic unity" or "primary unity", or as "primary object-relationship". Failure here results in the experience of *deprivation*. When analysis succeeds in repairing such failure, we see the phase of the "New beginning", as Balint has described it. Kleinian analysis of the paranoid and depressive positions seems to aim especially at the traumatic complications of this "oral" source phase of development. The instinctual approach can alert us to fantasies and sensations with specific qualities of complaints about Source, such as feeling of helplessness, or emptiness, of deadness, with anxious concern about damaged vital organs, especially in the digestive and respiratory systems. Effective self-provocative procedures may expose images of the SOURCE objects, mother, breast, home, and so forth, as being magical, monstrous, destructive, poisoning, refusing, omnipotent forces.

The source of an instinct is closest to the biological energy process, and its study is here confronted most seriously with the mind-body dilemma, and the difficult question of first transformations of "energy".

The term *"Aim"* has reference to experiencing a good sense of effort in the body pathways for *expressing the action* required by the instinctual function as a whole. Therefore, this involves a fuller attention to the dimensions of awareness about body sensations, especially of the muscles. The state of successful *Aim* processes has been classically referred to as "function-pleasure" and these processes may be most relevant to the controversial problem of secondary narcissism. Failure here appears to produce a variety of masochistic complaints, with images and feelings about being "tied up", "hung up", being forced into submission and feeling violated in one's natural or spontaneous pace of self-expression. One is reminded here of Winnicott's "spontaneous gesture," (1971) as an aspect of play.

These complaints about self-expression were especially typical of the experienced patients I have discussed. Perhaps it is to be expected that we will find many such difficulties in the character neuroses. The fantasied and actual trauma exposed by self-provocation procedures show a process of *suppression* by intruding objects. In some of these cases it has been possible to recover and reconstruct very early memories of oppressive parental supervision and intrusion into eating and excretory functions. More usually the evoked memories refer to more subtle forms of parental domination of the patient's early exploratory thinking and movements. The central crisis is a sense of being squeezed, and thus belittled and devalued while trying to express and experience a feeling of having rights and worth in function-pleasures.

The third aspect, the *"Object"* of an instinct, refers to the experience of completing the sense of effort in the exchange of instinctual tension. It is an active use of the external world to precipitate the discharge of the instinctual "energy". While we are not yet clear about the criteria of "tension", nor about the process of "discharge" of psychic forms or "energy", the object aspect of the instinct has been studied from the beginning of psycho-analysis in the phallic and hysteric defenses against the oedipal conflict. The term "frustration" is widely adopted for this type of trauma. We know its complications and compromises to include the retreat to problems of possessing object parts inside oneself and the problems of narcissistic preoccupation with one's own erotogenic ones. In current analytic practice we easily recognize these manifestations of frustration. It becomes necessary to add self-provocative procedures to free the patient to confront his still active trauma in the *aim* and *source* aspects of his neurotic ego-instinct conflicts, and renew his intent for reparation.

There are, of course, varying combinations of the experiences of *deprivation, suppression and frustration,* to be expected behind each major symptom confronting us in our patients. In fact, we're still far from being able to outline the complex, over-lapping patterns of the three aspects of each instinct. A fair presentation of a case would require a detailed statement of the exact sequence of these three layers of trauma and the working through of the transference complications from the self-provocative procedures for each phase. I now realize that this would take 2 or 3 hours, and require as much discussion. But we do know now how these instinctual aspects may each split off and therefore obstruct good, genital, mutual object-relationships.

Our analysis of the components of the instinct may permit us to note more fully the necessary roles of adequate narcissistic supplies and expression for more completely satisfactory object-relations, both woven into the ego flexibility of the genital character structure. This spontaneous wish to include the reparation one's narcissistic resources and pleasures, to be available for object-relations, is the first major theoretical implication I sense from the use of the principle of self-provocation with these experienced patients. It may follow that the analyst's transference analysis will be more specific to these patients' regaining of narcissistic capacities to the extent one possesses them, with analytic awareness, in oneself.

That 1963 paper originally included a detailed case study but Balint advised I remove it; it was "too provocative until the general principles are more familiar." I took his advice and published it later (1972) in a more developed context of theory. Following my presentation of this 1963 paper, Balint commented that even the British Society would not be ready to consider my hypotheses for some time, many years perhaps. He recounted the difficulties in obtaining any substantial consideration for his work, especially his latest book then, *Thrills and Regressions*. Within a year, I arranged to return to the United States, in fact, to move to Los Angeles, which I saw as a frontier of human evolution. The next chapter discusses some of the ideas which were developed in that phase. California living did stimulate some special rethinking of the concept of narcissism and its challenge to traditional analytic psychotherapy.

XII

Rethinking Narcissism

The classical myth of Narcissus, for all its variations, has been strained and changed in Western social history to meet the viscissitudes of the sense of self as our culture evolves. Jean Sanville has fashioned a telling tale about a "pseudo-autonomous male who poses as self-sufficient . . . perishing of anorexia nervosa" (Shor and Sanville, 1978, pp. 156–7). She describes his mother's overprotectiveness which "deprived him of that mirroring on which a cohesive sense of self depends." His lack of capacity for empathy and warmth rendered him unable to respond to the inviting nymphs while he sought self repair without feeling enough safe space. We can elaborate further possible dynamics.

A clinician interviewing his mother would have discovered that he was born a twin; his much beloved and charming twin sister had died in infancy. Mother concealed him from all the doting friends and relatives. He grew up in a nearly autistic state with a schizoid affectlessness; such persons often look very beautiful in their smooth unlined skins and non-expressiveness but are unable to exchange meanings and feelings. Surprised and fascinated by the lovely feminine aspect of his defended self in the pool and reaching to fuse into a wholeness, he grabbed for the image and drowned in his own undeveloped mental representation.

It is not clear from the literature why his twin sister had

died. Had the mother overidentified projectively and failed to respect or nurture the infant's separateness and autonomy? Where is her mate and the father of the children? The mother's hidden neediness and inner resignation to a lesser personhood make for a semblance of surface quiet and containment which depress and suppress the capacity for dialogue. The surviving child may then identify with this sorry image and roam about lost and bereft yet yearning for warm empathic exchanges and the impetus to enrich his own functional capacities for a separate self love.

Hanns Sachs, an attorney turned analyst early enough to join Freud's first circle of colleagues about 1910, did a study (1942, pp. 100–131) of the constructive role of narcissism in the cultural evolution of Western civilization; one may add the preconditions of our religious developments which favored the nurturing of positive identifications with the monotheistic divinity who is represented as gentle and loving.

The issue for our theory and practice is the sensitive balancing of both dimensions, closeness and autonomy, in a dialectical spiral adapting to the inner pace of the less mature subject. Within such a safe, good-enough relationship, he can expose and explore his deeper dreads of rejection and rages of destructiveness and work through a pace of accommodations and assimilations to his own fuller personhood ready for next levels of the spiral. Our emphasis on the primary dialectic implies an essential coexistence; we differ from Balint's view here that "Narcissism is always secondary" (1952, pp. 258–9, also 1968, pp. 40–45). We may be closer to Ferenczi's cues about "oscillation" between introjection and projection (1913). This alternating dynamic is proposed to characterize the mature stage of scientific thinking. We have added the hypothesis that the self, from the beginning, aims to attend to both dimensions, inner and outer resources and pressures; pathological narcissism is thus the product of a derailed dialogue.

This chapter is largely derived from a workshop presented by Jean Sanville and myself at the 1985 New York Conference of the American Psychoanalytic Association. The essentially joint authorship remains evident in the text:

In response to the recent polarization between object relations theories and self psychology, we are proposing a clinical approach which would attend directly to the details of patients' complaints as they reveal areas of felt difficulty or obstacles both to self fulfillment and to connections with other. The suggested theoretical framework derives from a renewal of Freud's original formulations about the phases of human "instinct" in psychic development: source, aim, and object. Further inspiration comes from certain concepts of the British "Independents," especially Balint and Winnicott, to do with play and illusion. Our clinical approach attempts to develop Freud's (1914) hint that the "battleground" of psychoanalysis is to be won in treating the "transference as a playground."

We find a cue for our approach from a tune which was popular in the late 1930's, and which was featured in a Hollywood film in 1944. It offers the *illusion* of three hearts all yearning toward a loved one, and it suggested to us a way of representing what we have thought to be three aspects of self-regard as well as three fundamental qualities of human relating. We propose to explore how the three dimensions or ego functions emerge in psychosexual development and how they appear in clinical practice:

Me, Myself, and I are all in love with you
We all think you're wonderful, we do
Me, Myself and I have just one point of view
We're convinced there's no one else like you.
   It cannot be denied dear
You brought the sun to us
We'd be satisfied dear
If you belonged to one of us
   So if you pass me bye
Three hearts will break in two
'Cause Me Myself and I
Are all in love with you.

> Song written in 1937 by
> Irving Gordon, Allan Roberts
> and Alvin S. Kaufman.
> In film *Atlantic Flight*, 1944
> starring Dick Powell

167

It is possible to view the development of psychoanalysis from around 1900 until now as a gradual but continuous "normalizing" of aspects of the human condition which were originally associated with psychopathology. Reading through Freud's early cases, we find him repeatedly insisting that his patients were not "degenerate," and he worked in the firm belief that it would be possible to make sense out of what must have appeared to many observers of that day as non-sense. To find, or perhaps to help constitute meanings in human data which seemed meaningless was indeed his life's work; thus the gradual expansion of the types of patients to whom analysts have been attending with hopes to find meaning and to develop methods for advancing developments which had been fixated or regressed. The dynamics which he found in the conflicts of his patients he assumed to be potentially present in us all; particularly did he view as crucial for development the "mechanism of defense" which are utilized to cope with the universal problems such as the oedipus complex. He alerted us to the ubiquity of symbolism—a special tendency of the human animal, both its glory and its downfall. In his writings on dreams, daydreams and on jokes and slips-of-the-tongue, he made clear the presence of the unconscious in us all.

Freud extrapolated from his brief encounters with children (such as Little Hans), from his adolescent females (Katharina, Dora and the "Homosexual Woman"), and from reconstructions in adult analyses, to develop theories about human growth and unfolding, with its ages and stages of psychosexual development, a schema on which we are still building today—extending it downward to the earliest period of life, and upward toward old age. For our purposes here we note particularly his assumption of a "primary narcissism," which over time must be "tamed" so that object relations become possible. However, we should also be mindful that Freud did not feel the necessity to make up his mind too absolutely about that early state, for he did posit that early identifications lie hidden in the ego ideal, identifications in the "prehistory of every person." And he did see (1925) that the next big task for psychoanalysis was to develop an adequate theory and clinical methods for narcissism in human development (XX p. 61). He had already given a clinical clue to the reparative aspect of narcissism in a 1914 article: "Perhaps it is only when the megalomania fails that the damming up of libido in the ego becomes pathogenic and starts the process of recovery which gives us the impression of being a disease" (XIV, p. 86).

In his search for better ways of learning and of treating, Freud found it important to relinquish to a large extent the traditional role of doctor. In his very first case study he reports Emmy von N's petulant plea that he stop interrupting her and listen; after this he began to be less authoritarian and gradually learned to attend closely to his patients' complaints and their ways of seeing themselves and their situations. He started to develop what some of us have subsequently seen as the basic ethic of psychoanalysis: a respect for the patient's own material, own autonomy and pace, and own capacity for growth and for development toward better solutions to life's problems—especially when equipped with the self-awareness which analysis can impart.

But some of what Freud regarded as "bedrock," the lowest level which could be reached by the spade of psychoanalysis, has been challenging subsequent analysts to develop sharper and sturdier tools—methods which would extend the range of complaints with which psychoanalysis might deal. Freud did not see analysis as possible with "narcissistic personalities" because such patients did not seem to be able to make a transference, as he then defined it, that is, as deriving from the oedipal conflict. He saw fixation at autoerotic and narcissistic stages as precluding object relations.

However, certain of his immediate followers struggled with this problem and began to offer glimpses into the preoedipal period. Ferenczi (1926) hypothesized the omnipotence of the infant, since events occur because of his cry and since he is unaware of the steps which occur "in reality" between his feelings and the ensuing actions of others. Magical thinking has its roots in this "golden age." Abraham refined notions of these early years, and developed concepts of six preoedipal stages: oral, anal and phallic, with a passive and an active phase of each. He saw character as a continuation of childhood fixations at one or another stage.

Melanie Klein (1955), taking her cues from Freud, Ferenczi and Abraham, based her theories on direct observation of children in analysis, and she pushed the search for understanding further and further back into earliest infancy. She contended that object relations were operative from the start, and that narcissism was contemporaneous with them. The first autonomous "judgment" of the child is that something is either "good" or "bad," and the infant can swallow or spit it out, or can bite! But that autonomy is qualified because the infant is buffeted by the death instinct, the strength of which is constitutionally determined. This innate aggressiveness enters into his perceptions of self and others; hence the paranoid position is the first phase of the baby's response to the world. As Freud had postulated the ubiquity of neurotic conflicts, she affirmed the ubiquity of anxieties of a psychotic nature in infancy. And she assumed the universality too of the necessity to pass through a depressive position, with its anxieties stemming from the need to see both good and bad in self and object. Her proposition, that the precondition for both a stable ego and satisfying object relationships is the "good internalized object", guides much of our practice today, including the theories and methods of some of the writers we are discussing—although they may or may not express their gratitude.

Kernberg (1975) sees his developmental frame as evolved from ego psychology in the light of object relations theory. His language is that of classical metapsychology; for him, *self* is defined as "an emergent ego structure that gradually centralizes major ego functions"—or, somewhat redundantly, he speaks of the "self as the integration of the self-concept." He imagines the primary state of the infant to be one of "undifferentiated self-object representation out of which narcissistic and object investments develop simultaneously," this being similar to Klein's view (although he is in many ways critical of her) and to Freud's undifferentiated ego-id, and to Ferenczi's "pre-object love." Like Klein, he sees the "inborn intensity of the aggressive drive" as predisposing to the development of narcissistic disorders, but, unlike Klein, he adds as part of etiology the actuality of "a cold, narcissistic and overprotective mother." Although he affirms that one cannot study the vicissitudes of narcissism without also studying the vicissitudes of object relationships, he seems to take a fairly pejorative view of narcissism, concerning himself mainly with its pathological forms. Even in his recent writings on love, he continues to be impressed with the universality and intensity of human aggression and its ever-present threat to close relationships. Especially is this threat evident in the relationship between the narcissistic patient and analyst, where the latter must be constantly counteracting the patient's efforts toward omnipotent control and toward devaluation of the analyst.

Kohut (1972) has declared the probable need for two (or more) theoretical frameworks; for him drive theory might explain Guilty Man but not Tragic Man. For that latter purpose he has evolved a "psychology of the self." *Self* he defines loosely as the "center of the individual's psychological universe" (p. 311). It is "not knowable in its essence" for it is "a generalization from empirical data." The self of the newborn baby is a virtual *self* (i.e., existing in essence though not in actual fact, form or name.) At least the human environment responds *as if* the infant had formed a self, and the infant is "fused" with the environment that does so experience him. He would, like Abraham, say that the baby is not helpless but powerful, but he formulates the reasons differently: "because a milieu of empathic self-objects *is* indeed his *self*." (249) He questions the usefulness to analysis of the conceptualization of destructiveness as a primary instinct striving toward its goal. Although "elemental aggression" exists from the beginning, it is more a "non-destructive aggressiveness" in the service of establishing a rudimentary self, and later it serves for self-maintenance. Destructive rage is always motivated by an injury to the self. Klein's "paranoid position," in his view, comes into existence only as a consequence of empathic failures; rage is "not an original sin, requiring expiation." Primitive, but not "psychologically primal," destructiveness is rather a "disintegration product." Thus, in analysis, the patient is not

171

confronted with a "bedrock" of hostility which he must recognize and tame. When destructiveness is manifest in the transference it is usually the consequence of the analyst's empathic failure or the activation of earlier traumatic experiences with self-objects.

As for the analyst's sometimes inadequate empathy, there is today a growing interest in the details and nuances of counter-transference, and especially in professional counter-transference, as manifested by subtle authoritarian stances in method (Balint 1959, Gill, 1982). Kernberg (1975), Kohut (1972) and others are hypothesizing about the "narcisistic personality," who has experienced such traumas too early and too frequently, and as a consequence suffers "structural deficits" which it is the task of analysis to fill in via "transmuting internalizations." Thus, although Kohut "brackets off" (as Schafer says) the self from the object line of development, and considers them as a "separate line," reparation cannot be accomplished alone. In fact, Kohut declared that the endopsychic narcissistic resources of normal adults remain forever incomplete. Absolute certainty about oneself and one's views is generally, he says, a sign of severe pathology. The healthy adult continues to need mirroring by self-objects, and also needs "targets for idealization."

Schafer (1976) would, of course, be critical of the metapsychological language used by all of the writers we have mentioned; particularly does he criticize Melanie Klein and "the so-called English School" for carrying "the reifications of metapsychology to a grotesque extreme." (p. 3) Self and identity are, he insists, ambiguous terms, having different meanings depending upon who is speaking; moreover, they tend to be reified. For him, *self* is "a thought, not an agent," or "a kind of telling about one's individuality;" it is a "mental representation." He suggests instead the word, *person*, by which he means "no more than is designated by I, she and you." (p. 217) It is the person who constructs the mental representations of self and of object. He assumes an "initially undifferentiated subjective experience of the mother-infant matrix," but would

172

translate Mahler's (1975) separation-individuation into the infant's acts of "representational differentiation." (p. 180) He hints that, at some later stage, the person might want to reverse that act; for instance, he says that in adolescence "representational cohesion" may be as important as "representational differentiation." (I assume he is suggesting some sort of imagined fusion.) As for innate aggression, Schafer abjures Freud's death instinct and its destructive energy; there is no "unlearned" knowledge of hating. Self-hatred is best described as the person's "own doing in the autarchic world of imagination and action on oneself." (1978, p. 125) Narcissism is defined as "consistently acting in certain self-loving ways in certain subjectively defined situations." (p. 137) And, with other "normalizers" he affirms that these acts may be done adaptively, defensively or self-destructively "in the fashion of Narcissis in the myth." Although Schafer denies that he is inventing new theories or clinical methods, only giving us back our "native language," if we adopt that tongue, it may provoke us to rethink "the future of illusion."

Shor and Sanville, in *Illusion in Loving* (1978) have postulated a "primary illusion" as a universal quality within the original state of the infant at birth—a gentle oscillation between an evanescent sense of self and an evanescent sense of other in dialogue. When all goes well, the infant has no felt need for "representational differentiation." It is only, as Freud said, "when the megalomania fails that the damming up of libido in the ego becomes pathogenic and starts the process of *recovery*," (italics ours.) In moments of felt deprivation, suppression or frustration in the baby, the good-enough caretaker tries to make appropriate responses, which is to say, responses that conform to the baby's own images of what would be reparative. Later, it is the therapist who, like the good-enough mother, has to help the patient to discern the reasons for the distress and to respond empathically. We have been attempting to delineate more clearly the qualities of patients' complaints as cues to their distress about "self" or about "objects," and as cues to the reparative fantasies which can be most valuable when they can be rendered conscious and capable of articulation. Then the patient can more effectively direct efforts at repairs "in reality."

Although we have borrowed from all of the writers we have mentioned, our vision is significantly different in certain important respects, and those differences do lead us to rethink not only language but also classical method. In some ways we may be temperamentally more attuned to Kohut, whose statement that "all worthwhile theorizing is tentative, probing, provisional—contains an element of playfulness" is one which we too affirm. "Ideals," he tells us, "are guides, not gods. If they become gods, they stifle man's playful creativeness" (1977, p. 312).

The Playground of Cultural Change and of Psychotherapy

Our thesis is that the narcissism, so much commented upon and written about in the Western world today, represents a broad swing of a universal human dialectic which characterizes both individual human life and the cultural life of human societies. Whether it is to be seen as constructive or as destructive will be to a considerable extent dependent upon the private or public context in which it occurs, and this context will modify the shape and manifestations of that line of development which we, perhaps mistakenly, globally term "narcissism."

It may be that only the Western world has developed a culture in which "narcissism" can flourish, only here that there is a great emphasis on the importance of the development of the *self*. And probably we can say that North America, even more than Europe, has placed high value on individuality and independence; we tend to judge our society and its institutions precisely by the yardstick of whether and to what extent they permit and encourage the equal opportunity of each person to develop his/her fullest potential through freedom of private choice. This is in marked contrast to many societies which, instead, measure the individual by the contributions he/she makes to the good of the whole, as the leaders define it.

The present authors have been working for several decades

174

in a part of the United States which may well constitute the zenith of cultures in which there seem to be few curbs on each person's "doing his own thing," where there is a high tolerance for non-conformity, for social experimentation of many sorts. We have thus been privileged to observe new human data, and no doubt our views have been stimulated by the particular sample of humankind with which we have been in contact. California is a kind of frontier, peopled by "immigrants" born and brought up elsewhere. The geographical space between them and their places of origin seems to translate into potential psychic space in which they feel free to try out many new forms of personal and social being, forms which would be looked upon askance in the more conservative east or midwest. The state is, as we read it, a sort of laboratory for the exploration of human possibilities. Hollywood, which turns out fantastic productions and dreams up heroines and heroes, has become for many the land of fantasy fulfillment.

Clearly not all Californians exploit these cultural leeways, and even among those who do, we are consulted by a relative few. On the non-patients we could comment only as do other arm-chair sociologists, so in keeping with our resolution to stay close to our own perceptions and experiences we have emphasized the clinical details with some generalizing of the concepts which apply to the therapeutic situation, concepts which we are continuously attempting to refine.

XIII

Psychotherapy Without Diagnostic Attitudes

Freud's *Autobiographical Study* (S.E. XX) could be read as his deepest statement about his life work. Here he is most humanistic in discouraging diagnostic attitudes: "It is left to the patient in all essentials to determine the course of the analysis and the arrangement of the material; any systematic handling of particular symptoms or complexes thus becomes impossible" (p. 41).

Since Freud's final normalizing of "a whole number of disturbances" (S.E. XXIII, p. 276) in idealized ego development, the British Independents (Balint, Winnicott, et. al; see Kohon, 1986) have expanded the humanization of psychoanalytic expertise with their ever deepening empathies for previously "pathological" experiencing. A most recent, and an exquisite, expression of this perspective is Bollas' chapter on "abnormal normality" (1989, p. 343); his literary penetrations may help to clear the professional atmosphere of the classical labelling exercises, while some of us try to fill in the fresh fertile space with our details about clinical practice. Yet the tradition of official name calling does not soften easily.

The last refuge of professional authority in psychotherapy may be its changing pronouncements about diagnostic categories as pathological pigeon-holes. Since the various labels for "neuroses" have been absorbed into the common language of our culture, competitive schools of therapists now feature new classifications such as narcissistic personalities or an evasive retreat to the "borderlines". Even these dynamic patterns will soon be taken over by Everyman.

I think psychoanalysis is in public trouble, its theories and its methods; it is in some disrepute in many establishment circles. Through all of my lifelong preoccupation and investment, I've seen serious critiques, fair and unfair, especially for the last two decades, from professional, academic, intellectual and popular forces (see Rangell, 1988). Sometimes, disillusioned patients publish personalized attacks on previous analysts (Strupp, H. H. 1982). We have some sturdy defenses. My favorite is in the conclusion of a previous joint book (1978):

> Psychoanalysis can play its part as a catalyst at the frontiers of consciousness, naturally and properly at the margin of conventional respectability to do its special work. Although only a small self-selective sample of people may choose to use this method, we guess that they are among those whose drive for primary love is the stronger and yet more harnessed to an equally powerful urge for that autonomy which can protect the illusion of fusion. The insights they gain are continuously diffused into social awareness through all the media of modern communication (Kris, Herma and Shor, 1943). . . . Psychoanalytic method is a catalyst for further evolution . . . (Shor and Sanville, p. 139).

A colleague on the faculty of Harvard's Psychiatry Department has been applying this perspective for over a decade of national responsibilities in meeting broad social policy problems. She has independently described her approach as "Creative Uses of Marginality." (M. Harvey, 1975). Psychoanalysis cannot properly function in the mainstream of culture since it specializes in repressed aspects of human experiencing; yet, by freeing awareness, it can enhance the texture of living.

A further defense I employ is to set aloft an exaggerated emphasis on playfulness in life, even for the serious works of building theories and treating patients in psychotherapy. We can intellectualize and then ask for a light regard for our peculiar notions. I keep a folder of stray notes which I label "A Selection of Freudiana Fragments for Fun" and I introduce the open listing with:

Here we indulge in a piece of regression to an old scholastic tradition in psychoanalysis. We will sift our way through Freud's writings to choose those statements which signify, to us, that he "really" meant to formulate the viewpoint which we have proceeded to develop. Our work is thus "validated" and our colleagues "must" attend; and this return to the *Source* is pronounced "constructive," if not benign.

Obviously, I've been exercising that device in some of these chapters and I've used many of the accumulating quotations at pointed places.

But if we listen well, especially to our experienced patients, we could make good use of some of the cultural objections. And if we look around at the proliferation of peer and self help therapy groups who selectively apply even our classical concepts and stereotypical aspects of our methods, our fresh analytic reflections and clinical testing may help to sift and refine society's suggestions. The major obstacle to such openness would be our tradition of authoritarian attitude as technical experts who assume a benign responsibility for helpless subjects, but neglect deeper potentialities or treat them as "resistances." This type of professional practitioner will have abandoned these essays many chapters ago. I have been reviewing some of our major traditional concepts and methods in the light of the general attitudes favored here. My emphasis continues to be on clinical details, not on formulating precise abstractions and definitions.

The troubles proclaimed against psychoanalysis in general have been changing their foci over the decades and we have sometimes fended off the various attacks with unanswerable accusations of unconscious "resistance," with interpretations derived from a sociology of cultural revolutions, or with an ignoring of critiques. Ernst Kris has classified many of the public rejections into three broad categories (1943, p. 329):

1. Deprecation through value judgments (ridicule, mockery, name-calling, moral disapproval)
2. Denial of the scientific character of the theory (methodology, verifiability, reliability)
3. Exposure of the social status of the theory (lack of originality, fashionableness, disagreements among "experts")

Kris does not counter attack with analytic interpretations. "Analysis is not suited for polemical use; it presupposes the consent of the person who is being analyzed . . . " (Freud, 1914, p. 49).

Our basic heritage is clearly not that of traditional science, however often Freud and others have hoped or intended (Bettelheim, 1984). Now there are signs that some hard science is seen to be softening its structural systems of concepts as in physics. Even *Chaos* (Gleick, 1987) illustrates the fruitfulness of attending to irregularity for new ideas. The sense of a comprehensive, firm, final plan in nature may be a useful but temporary illusion, a component of all playing. Our attention to feelings of safe space is a protection against a malignant chaos and destructive disorder. Yet a note of unpredictability may well permeate all human products including the shaping of all our sciences and knowledge.

In 1985, I participated in a summer seminar on "The Evolution of Evolution," at Oxford University, led by a very forward-looking biologist, A. Pomiankowski, a specialist in evolutionary genetics. He moved us through the official cliches to new vistas; for example, he freed us to appreciate that "ontogeny recapitulates misogyny." He showed us the loosened structure of hypotheses necessary for surveying the neural data presumed to underlie mental experiencing; a major reference for this perspective was the Nobel geneticist, Francois Jacob, who viewed the neural and immune systems as very subject to "flexible, non-genetic mechanisms" which evade closure (1982, p. 18). We discussed the courageous efforts of B. A. Farrell, who spent decades in the Oxford Philosophy Department trying to persuade his fellow "mental scientists" to leave open space for both common sense and psychodynamic hypotheses. And at the final meeting of our group, we studied the 1984 analysis of "Rules for Changing the Rules" by P. Bateson, a leading biological evolutionist at Cambridge University. Bateson concludes with this keynote:

> When we examine animals with nervous systems that were built with conditional rules for dealing with the external environment, the business of predicting how they will respond on the basis of knowing how they were made becomes impossible. It is like trying to predict the outcome of a game of chess before anyone has made a move. What we *can* do is attempt to get hold of the rules of the game so that we can make sense of a game as it is played. At that stage I concede happily that we may be able to predict what a clever animal will do in a particular set of circumstances. In the meantime, we should expect to be surprised very often. (pp. 503–4

We are not giving up our efforts to fathom the mysterious, ancient and new. But how useful are our diagnostic labels and evaluations of case histories today for psychodynamic psychotherapy? Less developed humans, especially those suffering stultifying rigidities from traumatic experiences, are increasingly recognized as potentially fluid and open, not fixed in old viscissitudes. Those persons belittled by felt catastrophes may be predictable until we learn ways to reopen the paths for their inherent forward moving; this is our professional task, not evaluating them for insurance companies and minimizing the complexities of social-political policies. Since a freshman university course in British history, I have often remembered Edmund Burke's statement, "Calamity is a mighty leveler", and I regularly have seen its relevance also to authoritarian role playing psychotherapeutic practices. And our precious theories of personality dynamics so often set limits to the flexibilities, neurally equipped, for the unpredictable. When leading philosophers, physicists, biologists, evolutionists and neurobiologists move to the views quoted, I have a fresh appreciation for

Theodor Reik's (1937) emphasis on the surprise experience and "the courage not to understand". And I hope for more tolerance for my anecdotes and less demand for fully formulated case histories.

I see disadvantages and dangers in fixing diagnostic frameworks for personal and social experiencing, especially to our patients when we approach them asking for case histories or formulating systematic theories for explaining their symptoms. The flavor of our usual scientific terms, like "concepts" or "techniques" or even "clinical," hardens our approach and our experiencing of the encounter and the exchange with the patient. We know Bettelheim's study of the unfortunate translations of Freud's original "I,", "it," and "over-it" for the classical "Ego," "Id" and "Superego" (1984); it is sad that Freud allowed English translations to stiffen his messages about the human "soul" in these ways. His nineteenth century idols of firm "Science," however, did not prevent or destroy the humanizing attitudes which recurrently shine through his formal clinical concepts for psychoanalytic "technique." We do not need all of Freud's gestures to feel nourished enough to advance further.

The presence of both perspectives, the "scientific" and the "humanistic," is explicit from the earliest decade of psychoanalysis:

> I am vexed by two intentions: to discover what form the theory of psychical functioning will take if a quantitative line of approach, a kind of economics of nervous force, is introduced into it, and, secondly, to extract from psychopathology a yield for normal psychology. It is in fact impossible to form a satisfactory general view of neuro-psychotic disorders unless they can be linked to clear hypotheses upon normal psychical processes. (Freud, SE Vol. I, pp. 283–4)

In my first chapter there are several quotations indicating Freud's translating his first ambition to a respect for the unavailable, subjective qualities of the patient's, everyone's, private experience. With *The Interpretation of Dreams*, he explicitly took a position "in conflict with official science, which was to be its destiny" (SE XIII, p. 69). We are each in charge of our subjectivity. The experiencer *may* perform the act of quantifying internal processes when he decides to "work"; he may often choose not to measure when he proceeds to love and play if he feels safe "enough." We can see Freud the scientist suspending the traditional scientific model; so also the patient and ourselves.

Freud's second ambition has continued as the hallmark of psychoanalysis, the linking of the normal and the "pathological" experiencing in qualitative ways. This is achieved in our attempts to develop our general theories of motivation, wishes and defenses—whatever the names: instincts, drives, principles, desires, *et al.* The social and clinical ameliorative effects of psychoanalysis derive primarily, I think, from the normalization or "neutralization" of previously "pathological" behavior and experience. The resultant broadening of tolerance relieves the pressure for compounding the anxieties about inner damages and deficiencies, and it also reduces the concerns about being rejected, abused and experiencing additional external discriminations. The prime example from early days of psychoanalysis is that of infantile sexuality. So also were the concepts of repression, aggression, trauma, and the varieties of parapraxes, all put into the range of normality. Balint (1959, 1968) has achieved this liberation for "regression." Erikson's work implies such progress for borderline states, perhaps. However, the past two decades of Self Psychology have already established the constructive values possible for the "narcissistic" processes in development. I have alluded to much earlier cues in this direction in the work of Sachs (1942) and Jekels (1952). For the "clinical" work, Balint's careful descriptions of responding to malignant regressions from "basic faults" (1968) are major advances for facilitating repair processes. The old diagnostic distinctions become less useful, and even are discouragingly disruptive and intrusive.

We rather can attend patiently to the complex currents of affect in our subjects, as we do for ourselves in the usual flow of self awareness that continues the course of everyday living. This is the ultimate "normalization" for problem experiencing. It is the core data of self analysis, which is increasingly recognized as the essential goal of our "professional" efforts. It may appear that I recommending the eventual abolition of psychoanalytic psychotherapy as a technically specialized profession for experts; perhaps eventually, but not yet. Meanwhile Ornstein "has given up the concept of technique and thinks instead of the therapist's responsiveness . . . (and) considers his mode of listening the same with all patients regardless of diagnostic category" (in A. Rothstein 1988, p. 206–7).

Having practiced in a section of our home most all of the time, my children would early become aware of my preoccupation with patients very nearby. When my daughter was about four years old, she confronted me with questions about what my "work" was: "What do you do?" she asked directly. I ventured to reply in simplified but authentic terms, roughly: "I listen to what they think, what they feel, what they're worried or unhappy about, and when they ask me what ideas I have to help them, I tell them how I think about their worries and troubles." She thought a moment and said, still somewhat puzzled: "Mommy does that too. So does Grandma. Are they psychoanalysts, too?" I admitted that they also were, in some ways.

Am I selling this professional work short? Freud's listing of the "impossible professions" (SE XXIII, p. 248), education, government and psychoanalysis, surely can be seen as an outline of the main functions of parenthood, which thereby becomes the original and ultimate impossibility. Yet both motherhood and fatherhood are currently changing, perhaps significantly, influenced by the same cultural forces which are modifying psychotherapy. Behind all these social expressions there seems to be an elemental model for human being and becoming as an open-ended reaching for safe space and inner structures which then will be transcended as not good enough. A dialectic spiral emerges for and through all caretaking employments. All these pursuits become outmoded and a new platform is constructed for fresh evolutions.

Is my thesis here such a pretension, a claiming of a next style or ethic in attending to the strains of the person emerging? There are surely many old and alternative editions of the

183

general themes I propose. I may be asserting merely a personal programme pronouncing my pace in the professional dialogue. I experience this manifesto as an attempt at renewal of ancient aims, not as an invention or creation. Yet it is clearly rooted in a particular history of developing a style of psychoanalytic practice.

Coming through our culture's heritage for refining diagnostic categories, with their clinical implications for analytic theory and method, I early took to heart the pathological biases which signify our clinical heritage. I then taught "Abnormal Psychology" as the perspective for psychology. However another tradition from academic psychologists, was developing in the universities and a tentative compromise emerged into my doctoral dissertation in 1948. In that project, I believe I began the transition from a focus on pathology and its diagnostic discriminations to the humanistic and normalizing position underlying these essays. Therefore, I present here the summary pages, previously unpublished, from that work, with its historical perspective and terminology of four decades ago.

New Goals in Psychotherapy

This dissertation is an attempt at a philosophic synthesis of the new concepts and hypotheses in modern psychotherapy concerning the meaning of "good adjustment." The data employed in this study are primarily the formulations of psychotherapists published since 1900 in the professional journals, monographs and textbooks dealing with the theory and practice of psychological treatment. The professional literature of related social and natural sciences is also analyzed when it provides data or hypotheses which bear directly upon the immediate problem of defining the nature of psychological adjustment. There are five chapters.

Chapter one introduces the general problem, the related literature, the specific questions about the procedure. The current popular concern with psychological disorder and psychological treatment is interpreted as an extension of the liberal-democratic traditions in American culture; democratic men are increasingly sensitive to their inner life, in search of a more fulfilling life-experience. Psychotherapy is here viewed as an old social tradition which is now being equipped with new scientific data about men. Yet the survey of professional literature indicates an over-emphasis upon comparisons of methods of therapy and a neglect of careful definitions of the goals of therapy. The specific questions raised here are: the variety of expressed objectives in psychotherapy, the theoretical and experimental supports for each type of treatment goal, the conflicting issues among the several types of treatment goal, and finally the attempt at a synthesis of these conflicts toward a philosophy of psychotherapy.

Chapter two provides a brief historical background for the current philosophies in American psychotherapy. Three major trends are analyzed: the Journal, *Psychological Clinic*, published from 1907 to 1935, Freud's Psychoanalysis, in his *Clinical Papers*, covering 1896 to 1925, and the early Mental Hygiene movement up to the middle 1930's. These writings are explored carefully for their changing definitions of the goals of treatment. The specific needs for a more systematic definition of adjustment are listed and demonstrated.

Chapter three presents the results of the comprehensive analyses of all current definitions of successful personal adjustment. Eight basic types of definition of adjustment are evolved logically through the gathering of experimental and clinical evidence. Each of these eight types is interpreted as the product of a particular approach to the human personality. Thus, defining adjustment in terms of *overt actions* leads to the implication that adjustment is the conformity to social norms. Defining adjustment in terms of *character traits* also implies that the existing social standards and ideals are precise, integrated and finally validated. Defining adjustment in terms of *clinical syndromes* assumes that the diagnostic labels describe man's inner life adequately. Therefore, the study of man's *feelings and emotions* is interpreted as a necessary starting point toward defining the goal of a richer life-experience. Then there are crucial refinements of the definition of adjustment in terms of the depths of personality: *psychic motives*, unconscious *per-*

185

sonality mechanisms, the *total psyche* (Id-Ego-Superego), and finally the principles of *continuity and change* in the person as he proceeds from each stage of emotional development to the next.

Chapter four is a methodological discussion of the dilemma of man's multiple value-judgments as a special obstacle to evolving a scientific definition of good personal adjustment. The science of psychology is seen as subject to three basic types of distorting motives, corresponding to the concepts of Id, Superego and Ego.

Chapter five is the attempt at a more personal synthesis of the new trends in the philosophy of psychotherapy. The results of Chapter three and the methodological issues of chapter four are brought together in an interpretation of the current goals of psychotherapy as intrinsic to the liberal-democratic ethos of Western civilization.

(And then on pages 191–193, the following outline of clinical problems, based on a two-year survey of students at the Yale Mental Health Clinic, is given:)

The eight levels are to be described with concrete examples of the patients' expressions of their wish for help. Some current [1948] theoretical approaches particularly relevant to each level will also be indicated. Psychology is far from ready to specificy therapeutic methods for each level. These are the aspects of personality which the clients say they want to modify, to feel better about, to understand:

1. *Overt Behavior Trends*
   Referrents: Specific observable motor acts (reflexes, gestures, deeds, and misdeeds, conduct).
   Examples: "I can't study," "I drink too much," "I stammer in class," "I masturbate," "I have a twitch," "I grind my teeth," "I'm impotent."
   Special Approaches: Various Behaviorists and Operationalists (Hull, Toman, Skinner, Guthrie), Early Anthopology and Sociology.
2. *Personality Traits*
   Referrents: Self-characterization by trait names, signifying a socially defined trend in behavior.

Examples: "I'm shy . . . (or) self conscious . . . (or) stubborn . . . (or) impulsive (or) dependent (or) feminine . . . ", "My problem is procrastination."

Special Approaches: Paper-pencil personality tests (Bern-
reuter, et al.) Rating Scales.

3. *Clinical Syndromes*

Referrents: Patterns of Traits. Larger summary perspectives about traits, and/or behavior, sometimes with reported feelings. (Psychiatric Diagnostic Labels, Personality typologies).

Examples: "I'm an introvert," "I'm neurotic," "I learned
I'm a Manic-Depressive, from my psychology test."

Special Approaches: The Forensic Tradition of Psychia-
tory: Jung's typology, Minnesota Multi Phasic Inven-
tory and other tests.

4. *Emotions and Feelings*

Referrents: Awareness of sensations and feelings—often
relating to overt behaviors, traits and/or syndromes
(tensions, fears, anxieties, confusions, depressions).

Examples: "I'm feeling inferior to my roommates," "I'm
uneasy with girls," "I'm afraid I'm becoming homosexual," "I don't know why I'm at college," "I can't stand
my laboratory instructor," "I don't know what I want in
life," "I feel helpless," "I'm no good."

Special Approaches: Rogers' Non-Directive Counselling,
Psychosomatic Principles (Cannon, et al.), Titchnerian
Introspectionism, most chemo-therapy.

5. *Motivational Elements*

Referrents: Statements about motives, needs, wishes, attitude and values underlying the syndrome, traits, feelings and/or behaviors. (Usually conscious drives, both
coherent and absent in character).

Examples: "I want to get away, travel, see real life," "I'm
not sure I want to graduate," "I must be independent
of my parents," "I want to be more successful with
girls."

Special Approaches: The Early Mental Hygiene movement, the *Psychological Clinic*, and the Child Guidance Traditions. Non-directive Counselling.

6. *Personality Mechanisms (of Defense and Escape)*

Referrents: Interpretations of hidden motives and relationships behind above five levels (less conscious dynamic purposes, needs and considerations in compromises).

> *Examples:* (Infrequent) "I blame my teachers but it's really my fault," "Nothing interests me here so I day dream all day," "I pinch pennies for no good reason," "I'm looking for an out."
>
> *Special Approaches:* Recent Mental Hygiene and Clinical Approaches, Projective Testing (Thematic, Rorschachn, Sentence Completions, etc.) Also, most psychoanalytically-oriented psychotherapy.

7. *Total Structure of Personality Motivations*

> *Referrents:* Anatomy of the psyche (Id, Ego, Superego) suggesting the fundamental cores or types of motivational forces (essentially unconscious).
>
> *Examples:* (Rare)"I'm always struggling to meet standards and requirements, but I can't enjoy myself in anything I do."
>
> *Special Approaches:* Most "Psychoanalytic" Approaches.

8. *Continuity and Change (Life History Considerations)*

> *Referrents:* Recognition of continuity and change in motives and attitude through earlier experiences and relationships which significantly influence the person in process of developing his Id, Ego, and Superego drives, the specific mechanisms, conscious motives, etc . . . (Life history as the source of the intensities and canalizations, the economy of the mind).
>
> *Examples:* (Very Rare) "It's been in-growned in me so much to always be on top in everything that I'm never satisfied with what I do."
>
> *Special Approaches:* Some Psychoanalytic Approaches.

The examples given in the above outline probably illuminate more the concerns of the selected population sampled in the Yale Clinic, than the general population. Some of the difficulties are particular to their cultural background. Others refer to special problems typical of this age group, the late adolescent and early adult grappling with the outer and inner demands of and his wishes for mature adult life in a special social setting. Nevertheless the several levels appear to be the basic approaches applicable to any problem in personal adjustment. A developmental perspective has replaced the emphasis on diagnostic classification, through the increasing sensitiveness to patient's complaints and desires and through newer depth psychological methods.

Cultural progress may be defined to include ever more qualities of experience which were previously assigned to pathology. The psychic unity of humanity will favor an ever richer texture of possibilities for personal flexibility, both public and private. For such developments, there would be more subtle negotiations and more sensitive empathies in our social and legal systems. Perhaps their interpretations of meanings in reality and fantasy will be freer of authoritarian role playing. Sharing and mutuality may be more available as fairness and concern for one another are more institutionalized socially. There would be more safe space for complaints and desires to yield deeper gratifications in work, love and play.

Today, the diagnostic tradition at its best has evolved with open ended refinements of structural theory for the intrapsychic dynamics. A leading representative takes the position that "The fate of psychoanalysis will stand or fall on the strength of its theory" (Rangell, 1988, p. 314). I have here attempted a balancing emphasis on the task of liberating new clinical data in a wider field of intersubjectivities encompassing both patient and therapist.

XIV

"Fair Shares and Mutual Concern"
(Balint)

About a year after Michael Balint's death, his wife presented a paper entitled "Fair Shares and Mutual Concern," "based on notes written some years ago, mostly by Michael Balint, some by myself. . . . The notes were made following long discussions between the two of us, over the years" (E. Balint, 1972). Here new questions are formulated as old issues are reopened. Beyond their already advanced positions they share their speculations about fresh data from early infant participant observations and from flexible group therapy dynamics. The notes recognize an increasing variety of constructive and defensive responses to the subtle psychic trauma from dissonant encounters only now identifiable. The paper also reports tentative suggestions which point up the ongoing tasks of refining the caretaker's measures in response to the subject's efforts to make better estimates of their own private subjective experiencing.

We may remember how Balint began his professional independence with a creative critique of his teacher's presumption in failing to respect *"that the amount of excitation, the degree of the tension, is actually determined by the patient himself"*

(Balint, 1932, p. 155, italics in the original publication). This message has clearly become my touchstone, and new meanings, practices and perspectives have emerged for me. I call it an ethical principle though this risks oppositions from conscientious consciences who wish to construct their own evaluative anchors. And why not? With open-ended, ongoing evolution, there is no final, universal form or model. But guideposts have been useful en route. Balint's final book (1969) describes in rich clinical detail how "therapist and patient can tolerate the regression in a mutual experience" (p. 177) in a last chapter entitled "The Unobtrusive Analyst." This respectful valuing of the person inherent in the patient can resonate in the details of clinical practice.

In a summary review of Balint's last book, I concluded:

> Balint's concepts of *primary love* and *basic fault* present specific and persisting challenges for clinical method to refine its appreciation of pre-Oedipal, nonverbal experience. . . . Balint has worked mostly alone in this area of constructive regression since 1932. . . . His less insistent style may not appeal to those therapists urgent for clinical instructions or theoretical formulae. (Shor, 1969).

After Balint's death, I returned to the U.S. and retreated to a small abode on Malibu beach near Los Angeles. Transitional to reestablishing a practice, I joined a medical clinic where a leading Quaker psychiatrist invited me to study his efforts at combining his medical measures with the spiritual ways of his Quaker heritage. For decades I had glimpsed the special social qualities in that tradition, its deep respect for fairness, sharing and privacy. As I attended staff meetings and Sunday services, it was very moving to see at work a generous spirit of mutual concern for the comfortable pacing and self-expression of pains and joys by each individual; each person was invited to relate any moments of discovery or wonder he may have experienced recently, or ever. Yet there seemed no pressure to give up one's silence or private preoccupations. Self pacing is cardinal within the easy atmosphere.

I had read Michel Foucault's *Madness and Civilization* (1965) which included an account of a Quaker mental hospital about two centuries ago, in England, under Dr. Tuke, who saw "the need for Esteem" and a "form of reciprocity" within the patient's "monstrous surface" and "visible animality." Whatever the current diagnosis or actual mental state, each patient was daily invited to appear for Afternoon Tea, "where the guests dress in their best clothes, and vie with each other in politeness and propriety . . . [all] are treated with all the attention of strangers . . . with the greatest harmony and enjoyment. It rarely happens that any unpleasant circumstance occurs; the patients control to a wonderful degree, their different propensities. . . . " I see here a therapeutic regard for the basic positive potentialities of the person hidden in the pathology.

Yet Foucault adds this critique of the persisting authoritarian stance in most modern psychotherapy, including psychoanalysis: "It would not be a dialogue. It could not be that until psychoanalysis had exorcised this phenomenon of observation, essential to the nineteenth-century asylum, and substituted for its silent magic the powers of language. It would be fairer to say that psychoanalysis doubled the absolute observation of the watcher with the endless monologue of the person watched— thus preserving the old asylum structure of the non-reciprocal observation but balancing it, in a non-symmetrical reciprocity, by the new structure of language without response" (pp. 249–251).

Foucault's analysis supports the principle that we owe a "non combative reasonableness" (p. 252) in response to the patient's every act, which is to be seen as a deep reach for reasonable exchange. Direct easy questions from the patient deserve a direct reply, while an uneasy approach calls to be met by gently recognizing the disturbing affect manifest. Otherwise we are still role playing as a magical authority whose function is to make secret observations and diagnoses. Let me call that unfair, a not sharing, and not a working together on the patient's messages of complaint and hope, overt and repressed. The therapist alone can best evaluate the fairness and concern in his own attitudes and behavior.

My Quaker clinic experience yielded me much evidence that friendly respectful caring concern may go a long way; however the intrusive medical element was the introduction of a low-dose electro-narcosis injection and minor electric shock after the physician persuaded the patient that such procedure would help achieve a benign regression; this, he hoped, could allow a new beginning for the patient's efforts to repair his life. I was asked to sit in and attend the complete process, with its very decent verbal exchanges before and after the light convulsion and half-hour rest that followed each electro-narcotic experience. I recall one patient who had been "maintained" for years after a long period of very disorienting and disabling symptomatology. Her family also expressed satisfaction for the treatment which kept her lucid and friendly. One afternoon after her restful sleep she stole into my office to whisper: "Is the Doctor really helping me? Will I never *really* get better?" I suggested she could ask the Doctor all about these worries and feelings. In my approach the patient always has the right to confront his hired ally; the therapist can come clean or should leave the scene with honesty. Such straight exchanges sustain the self-respect of the claimant, though with variable gaps when experiencing the invasive assumptions and pharmaceutical preoccupations of current psychiatric practice.

In 1986 I spent a term as a visiting clinical lecturer at the Psychotherapy Section of Oxford University's Psychiatry Department and enjoyed a long fantasied experience of living in an old College residence club. The pharmaceutical preoccupation was dominant in that large department, as remains true for most all of psychiatry in the U.S.A., yet our "Psychotherapy Cottage" was still open to free discussion of psychodynamic ideas in practices. Of course as an old Anglophile, I was disappointed not to see more of the Quaker spirit in the halls of the Academic Establishment. But I found it in a corner of the larger culture, the National Health Service. On a side street just off the main roadway, a little store front served as the entrance to a clinic supported entirely by the Health Service and volunteering professionals. I was invited to participate in staff case conferences on a regular weekly basis. It was a walk-in service; no names or identification were required, no fixed appointments, a free self-directing opportunity for any individual. The staff members were sensitively flexible in their approaches and they clearly recognized that the voluntary patient is to remain in charge in all details, as Freud has advised (1925). I found it a very moving experience, personally and professionally.

Several professional experiences during the past three years as Lecturer in Harvard's Psychiatry Department (Cambridge Hospital) gave further evidence of the cohesive and creative values of this principle of improving patienthood status by a fairer sharing of decisions and measurements in a partnership with the patient en route to the dialogue I've described for my analytic patients. One of my frequent functions for staff, interns and residents was to "do a conference" discussing and interviewing selected patients about whom there was uncertainty in status or for therapeutic planning, with all Staff attending. Even long term, backward State Hospital patients were reviewed through such a conference. These were opportunities for me to try out and learn the applicability of the purist, high-minded principles of patient psychotherapy about which I was lecturing and with which I provided regular supervision to self selected staff. Facing the challenge of the drastically diagnosed and impaired closed ward patients, I chatted with them about their feelings towards their immediate experiences; no case history or psychodynamic interpretations was pursued. Their often mechanical mumbling and apathy moved me to empathic questions about their apparently dulled and submissive states. They usually replied with fragmented comments about the medication just given to them. I pursued this theme to ask their estimates about the amounts and types of drugs being administered. Their interest seemed to awaken, especially as I dared to describe the possibility that the attending psychiatrist might regularly consult and discuss with them the choice and dosage, inviting the patients' regular reports of the felt effects each time; the two allies might work together in detail. In subsequent weeks, staff members reported to me significant changes in these patients' ward behavior and their attitudes about themselves. Some became more actively troublesome while others began to plan with their therapist for next considerations toward release and rehabilitations. In both cases, they were advancing from dumb accommodating toward an assertiveness which allowed for lively discussion of problems and prospects in the direction of bettering relationships and enjoying autonomy. I see these as steps, potentially, toward a therapeutic dialogue, whether we name it psychoanalytical or not.

In this postulated model of a dialectic spiral, changing would be likely and perhaps infinite in time. Yet we each can claim a pace that punctuates the oscillating flow between the wish for mutuality and the search for ever-greater individuality. Alternating between illusions of fusion and fantasies of absolute autonomy, we can fashion compromises in a spirit of fairness and justice, softened with efforts to share and exchange concern. We enhance ourselves and one another in this spiral when our separate paces meet in experienced attunements and resonances. Such good fortune is not more predictable in the chance combinings that make for the therapist-patient pair than in the "mother-child unit" (Winnicott, 1972). From the professional side, positive outcomes are favored by equipping ourselves internally for that openness in negotiation and empathy, and by sharing our learning with our culture at large, not simply writing for already like-minded colleagues or in hard, technical terms. But patience is crucial.

The best of psychotherapy will find its raw data in the never-finished realms of persons expressing complaining and desiring. This core data initiates the helping relationship and it also provides the criteria for properly concluding that connection most completely, for the present. The presumptions of the professional permeate the range and the processes between the beginning and the end of treatment; here is where we can facilitate or complicate the patient's inherent efforts, with his particular pace of discovering, measuring and choosing. As we

195

increasingly allow him to select and regulate all the details of the working alliance, he will invent and modify the procedures he feels he needs for his ends, as well as construct the terms, the words, the narratives and the explanations which best serve as the sieve of his entire experience.

Our professional language may be our private playing or our shifting shorthand in the tight contentiousness of competing cults and schools of thought; it must not intrude into the already delicate and wary doubts and distrusts residing in the client.

In an open society, which is a matter of degrees and domains, the culture will likely promote even disputatious consideration of the specialized formulations of technical "experts" in the human sciences; this is a useful and necessary form of dialogue at large. The public trouble in which psychoanalysis finds itself is a tribute to its felt relevance. During my several years in London, two decades ago, I was impressed that even our most difficult and complex psychoanalytic books were regularly reviewed in the middle class newspapers along with popular novels, literary criticism and sociological and historical treatises; all this pleased the anglophilic biases which I shared, secretly, with Freud (Jones, 1964 vol III).

Potential clients grapple with and also individualize the public messages available in preparation for and selection of their particular styles of patienthood. The more we respect their choices of ways of reaching for our help, the further and deeper they can learn and innovate, and then contribute to the common reservoir of alternatives for others. Their inherent capacities and wishes to share in fairness and to care with concern may more likely mature and enrich us all. All this derives from the pervading assumption that psychoanalytic methods and theories are primarily and ultimately the creation of the patient. Good ole Emmy von N. (S.E. II p. 63) and a few kudos to Freud himself; he explicitly allowed the patient to lead the way.

How this outlook can relieve us of some of the burdens and distortions, the iatrogenic transferences and professional countertransferences otherwise likely! But it increases our ethical responsibilities for our presences with the patient, who should remain essentially in charge. Invading those professional responsibilities, of course, are the private personal tasks for self regulation about which very little can be usefully said when uninvited. I remember how an "innocent" exposition of this view to a group of close colleagues led to their dubbing me, playfully I hope, "Mr. Superego," and I retreated into a shadowed corner, blushing. I had suggested that we all discuss our ethical principles for psychotherapy. The best of them remained friends, to be sure.

I am still searching for a better word for my term, "ethics." "Subjectivity" also runs the risks of absolute relativism and pure anarchy, which I feel I cannot afford, as yet. Better words and flexible narratives are necessary but sometimes not good enough. The humanist psychoanalyst can improve his listening and facilitating the patient's efforts to make and remake his narratives, *ad infinitum.*

Yet, these reports have been serving me as pointers to principles, as memories with mourning and as illustrations of models and motivation in anticipating further possibilities. The footloose mixing of these cues to work, love and play may be brewing a muddled recipe of variable taste and tact. I hope many more of my colleagues will produce their stews of complaints and desires, claiming their rights to own and revise their sources, aims and objects. The ongoing tales, like reparative narratives, can stimulate our dialoguing into safer spaces and fresh territories.

Postlude: On Complaints, Dialogues and Narratives for Self Repair.

The stories we weave about a life or about a perspective like humanism do change with time, but they remain interlaced with some hidden personal secrets and defensive ideas. The reshaping of privacy is in continual evolution, individually and socially. Cultural standards and psychic tolerances do modify the forms of safe space and free play. These shifts press the helping professions to rethink and redo their theories and methods. Major credit for progress belongs to protesting patients and flexible therapists, to those who share their complaints and are willing to discuss. The resulting dialogues, both public and private, evoke cues to stimulate researching and testing which can refine next levels of stability and of freedom.

The theoretical yield of this work derives from both a better listening to patients and the recent data on infant observation. We have come closer to a positive image of an innate open self reaching for both reflective autonomy and reciprocal intimacy. I have identified a primary model of dialogue as the ideal pathway for development, and some unavoidable disruptions which occur from experiences of deprivation, suppression and frustration. New recognitions of failures of attunement and resonance are emerging. I have proposed that some inevitable precipitation of three qualities of self or personhood occurs: ME, MYSELF and I. We are learning to rerail the primary dialogue by fresh sensitivities in negotiation, empathy and joint interpretation of hidden complaints and desires, all aiming for richer forms of working, loving and playing together. These terms have become the language of my therapy practice, always explicitly directed to the self reparative intentions.

The dialogue model is the main focus in this book, and it is applied in detail to illustrate the humanistic respect for the privately defined potentialities of the individual patient. The presenting complaints develop into reparative narratives with a minimum of resistant transference neuroses as long as the client remains in charge of the pace and procedures for self repair. I have described difficulties in the recommended sequence of negotiation, empathy, and then interpretation. Sources and cues to the spirit and methods of this open-ended approach to psychoanalytic therapy have been identified in recent professional literature. Increasingly our profession agrees that the ultimate goal of therapy is to become one's own analyst. I've proposed that this aim can permeate clinical practice from the first contact for all patients, whatever may be their initial complaints, diagnoses and desires. Yet, challenges were located in the ethics and maturity of the therapist. We are advancing nearer to the fulfillment of Freud's (1925) advice:

"It is left to the patient in all essentials to determine the course of the analysis and the arrangement of the material." (SE XX, 41).

We remember Freud's dialogue style, with his many hints of coming concerns, about earlier biological and infantile processes as well as about later psycho-social complications. In science, the spiral dialectic of evolution and development is ever-open at both ends of the time dimension. Historians continue to discover hidden forces and secret dynamics from the past while current neurological researchers and near mystical visionaries stretch our minds with tentative tales, promising and threatening, about unforeseen resources and possibilities. For this necessary "chaos" (Gleick, 1987) we need a stabilizing core for coherence of the self. Freud's heritage has yielded such a stabilizer in his speculative idea of a budding person who envisions no ultimate limits to omniscience and omnipotence. The gaps between such fantasy and reality are "liable to a whole number of disturbances" (SE XXIII, p. 276); here is our professional challenge.

The thesis here, so far, is a comprehensive set of working hypotheses: The natural development of human energies must move from primary scarcities of vital supplies and uncertain self expression towards sufficient abundances of goods and powers before the person can afford to lend its self to mutual exchange and flexible merging with loving fusion. The measures of all these qualities are deeply private and subjective, and when the quantities of felt supplies do not serve well enough, defensive compromises and symbolic substitutes are adopted. Fixations occur under special, severe circumstances of deprivation, suppression, and frustration, with a resulting anxious rigidity in the feelings for greed, envy and control, status or power over others. Repair of these conditions requires a renewal of a primary dialogue model through benign regressions, which contain the impetus for safe, easy abundance of supplies and self expression. Then, the original energies may move towards a richer fulfillment of all capacities to function in a context of responsive dialogue with the other.

From the first readings of Freud's major writings, I was startled by the fertility of a particular set of ideas which he proposed for the basic thrust of human psychological development, a series of phases in cultural evolution: the magical, the religious and then the scientific "systems of thought" (S.E. XIII, p. 77). The same year, 1913, Ferenczi's "Stages in the Development of the Sense of Reality", deepen Freud's terms with primary psychodynamic processes: introjection of powers in the magical attitudes, projection of powers for the religious, and combining these for scientific thinking. He also adds a fresh appreciation of symbolic regressive processes which qualify the past models for later contingencies. In 1926, Ferenczi explicitly advances Freud's basic dualistic approach into "an oscillation between projection and introjection" (p. 373) and he

200

prepares us for the dialectic spiral which we (Shor and San-ville, 1978) have translated into the primary illusion.

That series of phases, *magical, religious* and *scientific*, has specific implications for the changing roles of the therapist and the patient. The magical mode emphasizes mechanistic explanations and procedures to be given by the manager and introjected by the deficient sufferer; the successful physical sciences offered such manipulative models to early psychoanalysis with its "techniques". The religious framework allows the patient to project his paralyzed powers on to the awesome authority and gradually permits the subject to battle and confront the transference conflicts to gain and regain autonomy. The psychologically scientific attitude works to create a safe space, a playground, where negotiation fosters empathic closeness for a dialogue with joint interpreting; the therapist serves as a reflective, playful resource in flexible, responsive relating. I have hypothesized that primary self reparative wishes move the person along these phases through benign regressive efforts termed *self traumatization* and *self provocation* (Shor, 1972).

The bridge from this abstract theory to clinical practice has been made passable for me with the special help of Balint's forty years of careful, sensitive writings (1930 to 1970). I now hear the complaining self, the patient, as wishing help to move from the burdens of fixed magical and religious attitudes to the risks and responsibilities of free choices to oscillate flexibly.

While Freud increased in time his respect for the self feeling and self determination of the person, he remained shy about pronouncing self reparative successes in the patient. Bolder, Ferenczi declared early the "organism's attempts at self cure" (1908, in 1926, p. 26) but Balint called him down for intrusive interventions and insufficient "patient waiting" (1932, p. 156). Today, many of us are speaking out for consistent respect for the individual's hidden capacities for self repair and for his private pace and preferences in this pursuit.

Less clear or recognized is the presence of a positive primary model for the self correcting efforts of the person. Here the therapist is in serious danger of projecting private preferences onto possibly unforeseen discoveries by others. This is a delicate difficulty of subjectivities in working with patients, so vulnerable to the imposing promising implied in the therapist's authority. Perhaps we must share this uncertainty with our client and modestly attend to our own subjectivities, yet remain open to new ideas, which we each may try out privately. It follows that my most frequent response to any suggestion of interpretation or of procedures in treatment is "O.K., let's try it, if you'd like."

Consequently, our current theories of human development and our methods of therapy will likely be insufficient for a next generation. Freud came to free us of much of the burden of authoritative responsibility in his most public writings, as in his 1925 pronouncement to the judicial system in Vienna for the case of Theodor Reik:

> It is easy now to describe our therapeutic aim. We try to restore the ego, to free it from its restrictions, and to give it back the command over the id which it has lost owing to its early repressions. It is for this one purpose that we carry out analysis, our whole technique is directed to this aim (S.E., XX, p. 205).

Private emotional factors may obstruct respecting such freedom and self responsibilities personally as well as professionally. A good friend with many years of clinical practice and teaching managed to evade commenting to me on the humanist perspective I was developing. For one long, leisurely weekend together, I set this point of view before him fully and pressed finally for some responses. He reflected seriously for hours and then as he ended his visit, he admitted archly ". . . . but I do like to feel like a wise old man". It's my impression our friendship waned somewhat after that directed encounter. Perhaps the humanist principles developed will modify even many of our personal relationships in time, when we can afford them.

My major assumption has been that at birth we each claim an abundance and also an interest in enhancing our vital supplies and functioning by engaging in dialogue processes which can become a dialectic spiral that includes merging, fusion, selective internalizing and separating as richer and more capable. From "easy alert" states (Wolff, 1959), we move to interact and may thus earn a bonding that facilitates further autonomy and intimacy. As urgencies occur, the growing efforts may agitate or suspend the self; symptoms are precipitated. We either get better or worse.

Bearable compromises are more likely as we age. Then because of lesser "impetus" (Freud, 1905), the striving for enhancing dialogue is more easily fragmented into parts, such roles as grandparents or retirees, with diffused relating or with narrowly concentrated hobbies, old or new. Some of us may continue particular, specialized interests with an exclusiveness that frees us of unequal exchanges with others, especially younger, or more abundant persons. Some resignation is likely, in wisdom or despair (Erikson, 1959). Yet this decade of increasing elders is evoking greater efforts to extend the time and energies for new forms of autonomy and interaction at subtler levels of the dialectic spiral. No absolute ends or beginnings are accepted as final conditions of knowing and doing.

My clinical experience in applying this humanist ethic has been limited mostly to functioning adults in psychoanalytic therapy. Braver colleagues have dared with far more complex patients. The American Orthopsychiatric Association held a full symposium on *The Light at the End of the Tunnel: Do Patients with Schizophrenia Get Better in Old Age?* (1983 Newsletter, p.41). Let me quote from my summary as official reporter:

There is good news, from recent and current longitudinal studies in Vermont, Connecticut, Massachusetts, Iowa and three areas in Europe, that de-institutionalization of "chronic" patients may allow for "rather full recovery" rates, given sensitive and flexible community care and support services. Several classical stereotypes may now be revised; we have substantial evidence that there is no fixed course for schizophrenia, that deterioration is not inevitable. Rather, responsive respect for the person's self determination and private measures of pace and degree of change may foster high skills and satisfactions in living and work arrangements.

These happy results were found in over 50% and up to 81%, of the several hundred aging patients included in the studies. The panelists are refining their methods of "sharing caring" and followup, with hopes of even better results as we more fully understand the individualized processes of self recovery and self-rehabilitation toward new and unpredictable areas of fulfillment.

This optimistic message was challenged, and several potential dangers and obstacles were recognized by the panelists themselves as well as by discussants. May the emphasis on self-recovery discourage governmental support of material and professional resources? Will mental health workers become too casual and inattentive to the individualized ways of patients in requesting and testing the flexibility of these resources? Do large urban areas make for special problems? How can professionals deal with their own "burnout" and other "counter-transference" reactions to both the former and the new stances: the officious "benign authoritarian" medical model and the highly personal involvements of "sharing caring" and decision processes? In the discussion of many of these issues, it was recognized that the professionals must particularly respect and attend to their own personhood.

Most impressive were the statistical and case data that, given a chance, these formerly back-ward subjects will reach, if cautiously, for a sense of dignity, independence and private self-regulation. Both patients and panelists have found less use for routine hospitalizations, drugs, "categories" of pathology and diagnostic labels. Even the recent discoveries about brain-biochemical defensive and reparative processes may be refined if professionals share with patients their questions and approaches to the testing of new drugs and invite and attend to the subjective reports of those who take them.

Freud can be credited with advancing these trends toward self-determination, although some orthodox analysts and psychiatrists have fostered subtly authoritarian attitudes. If the patient can feel safe to ask and discuss trying out drugs and to use brief hospitalization periods as "moratoria" to put self together before next efforts, both he/she and the physician can gain. The previously derailed processes of recovery can find their individualized ways back to "normalcy plus."

But this manuscript ends with a hope that new projects will be undertaken soon, much as the newborn looks about, inside and outside. The best current narratives may serve for a while, but persons who are mostly anxious from persisting failures of that primary illusion, felt as fixed, insist on hearing or telling ancient tales repetitiously. The repetitions may well aim for a next reparative turn, but there are uncertainties, even fresh threats, as we advance in age or cultural progress. So the spiral may turn in on itself for safety, but also for renewal. The present terms, like regression, dialogue and empathy, do get overburdened so that the language of self expression and of interaction moves to strange sounds and unfamiliar places. We will welcome the new work, the enduring love, the adventurous play.

The ongoing efforts at self repair are becoming implicit in the idea of self analysis which, most all analysts and therapists agree, is the goal of dynamic psychotherapy. Although these colleagues differ in their optimism and in their practice, such differences are rarely discussed openly. The few exceptions are noted in several of these essays. I suggest that these variables are hidden in the qualities of empathy offered to the patient. Since empathy alludes mostly to less verbalized feelings, there is more likelihood of imprecision and inaccuracy. The resonance is more faulty, yet the patient may respond to the hint that the therapist is reaching to his private experiencing. The patient may resist the intrusion or he may submit to the therapist's projection. This problem continues to challenge us in the task of offering gentle tentative hypotheses with a fuller alertness to imperfect resonance and attunement, much as the ideal mother may seek.

The therapist's personal readiness to refine his sensitivity to these unverbalized affects is at the heart of the empathy challenge, but this subject remains fairly taboo in our professional training institutes. Freud credited Ferenczi with the first suggestion that the analyst be well analyzed (Freud, S.E. XXIII, pp. 247–8). This touchy theme runs underground and gives rise to various forms of gossip, cynicism and sometimes gross attacks on the theories expounded publicly.

The patient's complaints and self interest are a useful protection and a valuable provocation to refine and revise the therapist's approach in his work. The new researches into infant interactions with the caretaker are also significant stimuli for improvements in therapeutic approach eventually. The reach for self repair continues to revitalize our explanatory narratives and to test the effectiveness of our clinical dialogues for freeing new possibilities of discovery and reflective autonomy.

As this humanist approach influenced my thinking and I gradually changed my ways of practice in details, I would remember clinical moments with former patients and wish I might call them back to share my new insights. Some of them did return on their own initiative for further work, love and play together. Since we are each the ultimate experts for our private experience, with the stimulus of ongoing self analysis, we can wish to share our fresh understandings and discoveries. The dialogues will go on amongst us.

References and Citations

[Numbers in brackets indicate the pages in this book where the work is cited.]

Arlow, J. A. and Brenner, C. (1988) "The Future of Psychoanalysis" *Psychoan. Quart.* V 57 (1). [114]

Atwood, G. C. and Stolorow, R. D. (1984) *Structures of Subjectivity*, N.J.: Analytic Press. [28]

Balint, E. (1972) "Fair Shares and Mutual Concern" *Int. J. Psychoan.* V. 53. [190]

Balint, M. (1932) "Character Analysis and New Beginning" in *Primary Love and Psychoanalytic Technique*, N.Y.: Liveright (New and Enlarged Edition, 1965). [6, 10, 18, 26, 140, 191]

Balint, M. (1933) "Dr. S. Ferenczi as Psychoanalyst" in *Problems of Human Pleasure and Behavior*, London: H. Karnac, 1987. [140, 191]

Balint, M. (1952) *Primary Love and Psychoanalytic Technique*, N.Y.: Liveright. [6, 11, 14, 44, 166]

Balint, M. (1959) *Thrills and Regressions*, N.Y.: Intern. Univ. Press. [16, 27, 37, 44, 54, 90, 140–144, 164]

Balint, M. (1967) "Sandor Ferenczi's Technical Experiments" *Psychoanalytic Techniques*, Edit. B. B. Wolman, N.Y.: Basic Books. [140, 191]

Balint, M. (1969) *The Basic Fault—Therapeutic Aspects of Regression*. London: Tavistock Publications. [7, 30, 34, 191]

Bateson, P. (1984) "Rules for Changing Rules" in *From Molecules to Man*, (Edit. R. Budel), Cambridge Press. [180]

Berger, D. M. (1987) *Clinical Empathy*, N.J.: Jason Aronson. [38]

Bergler, E. (1949) *The Basic Neurosis*, N.Y.: Grune & Stratton. [109]

Bergler, E. (1949a) "Freud on Creativity" *American Imago*. [117–118]

Bettleheim, B. (1984) *Freud and Man's Soul*, N.Y.: Random House. [92, 181]

Bion, W. R. (1967) *Second Thoughts*, N.Y.: Jason Aronson. [74]

Bion, W. R. (1977) *Seven Servants*, N.Y.: Jason Aronson. [74]

Blatt, S. J. and Behrends, R. S. (1987) "Internalization, Separation, Individuation and the Nature of Therapeutic Action," *Int. J. Psychoan.*, V. 68. [15, 20, 29, 42]

Bollas, C. (1987) *The Shadow of the Object*, London: Free Association Books. [176]

Bollas, C. (1989) "Normatic Illness" in *The Facilitating Environment*, (Edit. M. Fromm and B. Smith). New York: Intern. University Press. [176]

Caruth, E. C. (1988) "On Game as Play and Play as Game", *Psychoan. Psychol.*, V. 5 (2). [114]

Casement, P. (1985) *On Learning from the Patient*, London: Tavistock. [13]

Coleman, M. and Shor, J. (1953) "Ego Development Through Self-Traumatization", *Psychoanalytic Review*, V. XL, No. 3. [61, 66, 146–147]

Darwin, C. (1871) *The Descent of Man*, N.Y.: Modern Library. [16]

Darwin, C. (1872) *The Expression of Emotions in Man and Animals*, Chicago University Press. [20, 94, 145–146, 149, 154–160]

Davis, M. and Wallridge, D. (1982) *Boundary and Space: An Introduction to the Work of D. W. Winnicott*, London: Karnac. [44, 52]

Dewald, P. (1972) "The Clinical Assessment of Structural Change", *J. A. P. A.*, V. 20, no 2. [68]

Diamond, M. (1988) *Enriching Heredity*, N.Y.: Free Press (Macmillan). [30]

Eigen, M. (1989) "Aspects of Omniscience" in *The Facilitating Environment* (Edit. M. Fromm and B. Smith) N.Y.: Intern. Univ. Press. [33]

Eissler, K. R. (1965) *Medical Orthodoxy and the Future of Psychoanalysis*, N.Y.: Int. Univ. Press. [37, 78]

Erikson, E. H. (1950) *Childhood and Society*, N.Y.: W. W. Norton, Revised 1963. [31, 74]

Erikson, E. H. (1959) *Identity and the Life Cycle*, N.Y.: Int. Univ. Press. [8, 182, 203]

Erikson, E. H. (1964) *Insight and Responsibility: Ethical Implications of Psychoanalytic Insight*, N.Y.: W. W. Norton. [43, 74]

Fairbairn, R. D. (1953) *Psychoanalytic Study of the Personality*, London: Tavistock Press. [42]

Farrell, B. A. *The Standing of Psychoanalysis*. Oxford Univ. Press. [179]

Ferenczi, S. (1922) *First Contributions to Psychoanalysis*, London: Hogarth Press. [7]

Ferenczi, S. (1926) *Further Contributions To Psychoanalysis*, London: Hogarth Press. [17, 26, 169, 200]

Ferenczi, S. (1933) *Clinical Diary*, Edit. J. Dupont, Transl. M. Balint and N. Z. Jackson, Harvard Univ. Press (1987). [8]

Ferenczi, S. (1955) *Final Contributions to Psychoanalysis*, Ed. M. Balint, London: Hogarth Press. [201]

Fischer, R. (1987) "On fact and fiction" in *J. Social Biol Struct*, V. 10. [8]

Fiske, D. W. and Maddi, S. R. (1962) Edit. *Functions of Varied Experiences*, Ill: Dorsey Press. [14]

Foucault, M. (1965) *Madness and Civilization*, Vintage edit 1973. [192–193]

Frank, F. W. and Treichler, R. A. (1989) *Language, Gender and Professional Writing*, N.Y.: Modern Language Association. [41]

Freud, S.—All references to Freud's writings are specified in the text with their locations in the Standard Edition, in "S.E."

Fromm, M. G. and Smith, B. L. (Edit 1989) *The Facilitating Environment* N.Y. Int. Univ. Press. [69]

Gill, M. (1982) *The Analysis of the Transference*, N.Y.: Int. Univ. Press. [15, 28, 43, 65, 95]

Gill, M. (1988) "Converting Psychotherapy into Psychoanalysis" *Contemp. Psychoan.* V. 24 (2). [15, 28, 43, 129]

Gleick, J. (1987) *Chaos-Making a New Science*, New York: Viking. [179, 199]

Goldberg, A. (1987) "Psychoanalysis and Negotiation" *Psychoan Quarterly*, V. LVI. [15, 36]

Greenacre, P. (1956 and 1959) *Emotional Growth*, V. I and II, New York: Intern. Univ. Press. [14, 44]

Grolnick, S. (1978) *Between Reality and Fantasy*, London and N.Y.: Jason Aronson. [11]

Gustafsen, J. (1976) "The Mirror Transference in the Psychoanalytic Psychotherapy of Alcoholism" *Inten. J. Psychoanalytic Psychotherapy* V. 5. [127]

Hack, M. (1975), Film, *The Amazing Newborn*, Ohio: Case Western Reserve University. [15, 43]

Harvey, M. and Passy, L. (1978) "The Creative Uses of Marginality" *J. of Alternat. Human Servies* (4) [177]

Havens, L. (1986) *Making Contact: the Uses of Language in Psychotherapy* Harvard Univ. Press. [15, 64, 89]

Hobson, J. H. (1988) *The Dreaming Brain*, N.Y.: Basic Books. [99]

Huizinja, J. (1944) *Homo-Ludens: The Play Element in Culture*, Beacon Paperback, 1955. [52]

Jacob, F. (1982) *The Possible and the Actual*, Pantheon Books. [179]

Jekels, L. (1952) *Selected Papers* N.Y.: Intern Univ. Press. [73, 118, 182]

Kaplan, D. M. (1989) "The Place of the Dream in Psychotherapy" *Bull. Meninger Clinic.* V. 53. [100]

Kernberg, O. (1985) *Severe Personality Disorders* N.Y.: Basic Books. [15, 170]

Kestenberg, J. S. (1975). *Children and Parents*. N.Y.: Jason Aronson. [44]

Kohon, G. (edit) (1986) *The British School of Psychoanalysis: The Independent Tradition* London: Free Association Press. [10, 22, 88, 119–120]

Kohut, H (1971) *Analysis of the Self*, N.Y. Int. Univ. Press. [43, 47, 171–172]

Kohut, H. (1977) *Restoration of the Self* N.Y.: Int. Univ. Press. [15, 37, 67, 174]

Kohut, H. (1984) *How Does Analyses Cure?* Univ. of Chicago Press. [127]

Kris, E., Herma, J. and Shor, J. (1943). "Freud's Theory of the Dream in American Textbooks" in J. Abn. and Soc. Psychol. V. 38. No. 3. [23, 98, 107, 179]

Kris, E., (1975) *Selected Papers*, New Haven: Yale Univ. Press. [119]

Lazare, A., Eisenthal, S. Wasserman, L. (1975) "The Customer Approach to Patienthood", *Arch. Gen Psychiatry* V. 32. [15, 34, 79]

Lazare, A. and Eisenthal, S. (1988) "A Negotiated Approach to the Clinical Encounter *Outpatient Psychiatry* (In Press). [15]

Leavy, S. A. (1980) *The Psychoanalytic Dialogue* New Haven and London: Yale University Press. [15]

Lichtenberg, J., Bornstein, M. and Silver, D. (Editors) (1984) *Empathy,* Hilldale, N.J.: The Analytic Press. [65]

Loewald, H. (1970) "Psychoanalytic Theory and the Psychoanalytic Process" in *Psychoan. Study of the Child* V. XXV [28]

Loewald, H. (1978) *Psychoanalysis and the History of the Individual* New Haven: Yale University Press. [28, 43]

Loewald, H. (1988) *Sublimation,* New Haven: Yale Univ. Press. [43]

Margulies, A. (1984) "Toward Empathy: The Uses of Wonder", *Am J. Psychiatry* V. 141. [38]

Meissner, W. M. (1979) "Internalization and Object Relations" *J.A.P.A.* V. 27(2). [114]

Menninger, K. (1958) *Theory of Psychoanalytic Technique* N.Y.: Basic Books. [33, 114]

Milman, S. and Goldman, D. (1987) Techniques of Working with Resistance. N.J. Jason Aronson, Inc. [110, 128]

Milner, M. (1937) *An Experiment in Leisure* London, Virago Press 1986. [14]

Milner, M. (1956) "The Yell of Joy", Int. J. Psychoan. [14]

Milner, M. (1969) *The Hands of the Living God,* N.Y.: Intern Univ. Press. [14]

Milner, M. (1987) *The Supressed Madness of Sane Men,* London: Tavistock Publications. [14]

Milner, M. (1987a) *Eternity's Sunrise* London: Virago Press. [14, 17]

Modell, A. H. (1984) *Psychoanalysis in a New Context,* N.Y.: Intern. Univ. Press. [114]

Modell, A. H. (1985) "Self Preservation and the Preservation of the Self" in *Annual of Psychoanalysis* V. 12–13. [114]

Ornstein, P. (1988) "Multiple Curative Factors and Processes" in *How Does Treatment Help?* Edit. A Rothstein, N.Y.: State Univ. Press. [36]

Pedder, J. R. (1988) "Termination Reconsidered." *Int. J. Psychoan.* V. 69 (4). [68]

Peirce, C. S. (1923) *Chance, Love and Logic,* N.Y.: Harcourt Brace. [14]

Pert, C. B. (1986) "The Wisdom of the Receptors: Neuropeptides, the Emotions, and Bodymind" in *Advances* V. 3. [96, 112]

Pribram, K. (1971) *Languages of the Brain,* N.Y.: Prentice Hall. [21]

Rangell, L. (1988) "The Future of Psychoanalysis." *Psychoan. Quarterly* V. 57. [17, 189]

Reik, T. (1937) *Surprise and the Psychoanalyst—On the Conjecture and Comprehension of Unconscious Processes* London: Kegan Paul. [25, 28, 61, 74, 116, 119, 122, 131–135, 139–143]

Reik, T. (1948) *Listening with the Third Ear* N.Y.: Farrar Strauss—Arena Book. [116, 132]

Repko, G. R. (1973) *A Study of the Initial Dream in Therapy—The Forced and the Spontaneous Dream Report* Ph.D. Dissertation Calif. School of Professional Psychology. [99, 102–104]

Rothstein, A. (Edit) (1988) *How Does Treatment Help?* N.Y. Int. Univ. Press. [36, 183]

Sachs, H. (1942) *The Creative Unconscious* Cambridge, MA: Sci Art Publisher. [166, 182]

Sanville, J. (1979) *The Play in Clinical Education*—(250 pp.) Dissertation—International College. [10]

Sanville, J. (1979a) "Gentlemen Bountiful: Repairing the Patriarch" *CSWJ* 7(1). [10]

Sanville, J. (1982) "Partings and Impartings: Toward a Non-Medical Model of Interruptions and Terminations" *CSWJ* 10(2). [10]

Sanville, J. (1987) "Creativity and the Construction of the Self" *Psychoanalytic Review* 74(2). [10]

Schafer, R. (1976) *A New Language for Psychoanalysis* New Haven—Yale Univ. Press. [72, 172–173]

Schafer, R. (1983) *The Analytic Attitude* N.Y. Basic Books. [172–173]

Scheibel, A. (1989) *The Neurobiology of Higher Cognitive Functions* N.Y. Guilford Press. [30]

Schwaber, E. (1983) "Psychoanalytic Listening and Psychic Reality" *Int. Rev. Psychoan* V. 10. [114]

Schwaber, E. A. (1986) "Reconstruction and Perceptual Experience: Further Thoughts on Psychoanalytic Listening", *J.A.P.A.* V. 34, No. 4. [114]

Shor, J. (1939) "An Experiment in Individualism" in *J. Social Studies* Vol I, No. 1. [7]

Shor, J. (1948) *Changing Goals of Psychological Treatment* Dissertation—New York University and Library of Congress. [14, 24, 86, 108, 184–188]

Shor, J. (1953) "A Well-Spring of Psychoanalysis" in *Psychoanalysis—Journal of Psychoanalytic Psychology* (Now, *Psychoanalytic Review*) Vol. 2, No. 1. [120, 147–8]

Shor, J. (1953a) "Mastering the Dualistic Dilemma—Review of Jekels". *Psychoan Rev* V. 2. [76]

Shor, J. (1954) "Female Sexuality—Aspects and Prospects" in *Psychoanalysis—Journal of Psychoanalytic Psychology* (Now, *Psychoanalytic Review*) Vo. 2, No. 3. [18, 67, 71, 79, 90]

Shor, J. (1961) "The Ethic of Freud's Psychoanalysis" in *Int. J. Psychoan.* Vol XLII Part I–II. [76, 143, 148]

Shor, J. (1962) "Sources for Psychoanalysis in the Writings of Charles Darwin" presented to the *Imago Society*, London. [146]

Shor, J. (1963) "Self Provocation and Reparation" presented to *British Psycho Analytic Society*. [13]

Shor, J. (1963a) "Charles Darwin—Grandfather of Modern Psychotherapy," in *Intern. Mental Health Newsletter* Vol. V, Spring 1963. [16, 35, 95]

Shor, J. (1969) "Primary Love—Primary Illusion" in *Contemp. Psychology* Vol 14, No. 7. [7]

Shor, J. (1970) "Human Male or Human Being?" in *Psychiatry and Social Science Review* Jan 1970. [16, 40]

Shor, J. (1972) "Two Principles of Reparative Regression: Self Traumantization and Self-Provocation" in *Psychoan Review* V. 59, No. 2. [13, 72, 114, 201]

Shor, J. (1977) "Two Biases in Psychotherapy: Ocnophilia and Philobalism" presented to LA Society of Clinical Psychologists, June 1977. [72, 114]

Shor, J. (1985) "Dialogues from Infancy"—Essay Review of R. Spitz's Lifework—*Psychoanalytic Psychology* Vol 2(2). [10, 23]

Shor, J. and Frankel, W. (1939) "Looking for the Social Man" in *J. Social Studies* Vol I, No. 1. [7]

Shor, J. and Sanville, J. (1978) *Illusion in Loving:* A Psychoanalytic Approach to the Evolution of Intimacy and Autonomy Int. Univ Press 1978, and Penguin Paperback 1979. [5, 7, 15, 17, 22, 41, 46, 165, 173–174, 201]

Shor, J. and Sanville, J. (1985) "Bridging Self Psychology and Object Relations Theory" Workshop, Annual Conference, American Psychoanalytic Association. N.Y. [28]

Spitz, R. A. (1957) *No and Yes*—on the genesis of human communication. N.Y. Int. Univ. Press. [134]

Spitz, R. (1963) "The Evolution of the Dialogue" in *Drives, Affects and Behavior* M. Schur (Edit) NY: Int. Univ. Press. [7, 26, 46]

Spitz, R. (1964) "The Derailment of Dialogue" *JAPA* V. 12. [87]

Spitz, R. (1965) *The First Year of Life* N.Y.—IUP. [47]

Spitz, R. (1984) *Dialogues Fron Infancy* Ed. R. N. Emde—IUP—NY. [15, 21, 95]

Stern, D. S. (1985) *The Interpersonal World of the Infant* N.Y.: Basic Books. [15, 31, 43]

Stolorow, R. D. and Lachmann, F. M. (1984) "Transference: The Future of an Illusion", *Annual of Psychoanalysis,* V. 12–13. [28]

Stone, C. D. (1971) "Existential Humanism and the Law" in *Existential Humanistic Psychology,* T. Greening, ed., Brooks/Cole. [16]

Stone, L. (1961) *The Psychoanalytic Situation,* NY: Int. Univ. Press. [28, 43]

Stone, L. (1981) "Non-interpretive Elements in Psychoanalysis" *J.A.P.A.* V. 29. [28, 43]

Strupp, H. H. (1982) "Psychoanalytic Failure" in *Contemporary Psychoanalysis* Vol 18(2). [177]

Sutherland, J. D. (1980) "The British Object Relations Theorists: Balint, Winnicott, Fairborne, Guntrip" *J.A.P.A.,* V. 28 No. 4. [119–120]

Szasz, T. (1986) "The Case Against Suicide Prevention" *Amer. Psychologist* 1986 (July). [35]

Thomas, W., and Znaniecki, F. (1918) *The Polish Peasant,* University of Chicago Press. [4]

Trevarthan, C. (1984) "Emotions in Infancy: Regulators of Contact and Relationships with Persons" in *Approaches to Emotion* by Scherer, K. R. and Ekman, P. (Edits) Hillsdale, N.J. Lawrence Erdbaum Assoc. Publ. [15, 20, 43]

Tronick, E. Z. (1982) (Edit) *Social Interchange in Infancy:—Affect, Cognition and Communication* Baltimore: University Park Press. [43]

Winnicott, D. W. (1971) *Playing and Reality* N.Y.: Basic Books. [13, 44, 52, 195]

Winnicott, D. (1986) *Holding and Interpretation* London-Hogarth Press. [88]

Wolff, P. E. (1959) "Observations on newborn infants" *Psychosomatic Medicine,* V. 21. [14, 43, 92, 203]

Zinberg, N. E. (Edit) (1977) *Alternate States of Consciousness,* New York: MacMillan. [22]

Zinn, W. M. (1988) "Doctors Have Feelings Too" *J.A.M.A.* (6/10/88) V. 259 No. 22. [21]